Social Media Guide For Mortgage Brokers

How to Grow Your Brand on Social Media

Rosalia Lazzara-Tilley

Social Media Guide For Mortgage Brokers
How to Grow Your Brand on Social Media

ISBN: 9798856675275 Paperback

Published by: Inspired By Publishing

Cover Designed By: Tanya Grant, The TNG Designs Group Limited

The strategies in this book are presented primarily for enjoyment and educational purposes. Every effort has been made to trace copyright holders and obtain their permission for the use of copyright material.

The information and resources provided in this book are based upon the authors' personal experiences. Any outcome, income statements or other results, are based on the authors' experiences and there is no guarantee that your experience will be the same. There is an inherent risk in any business enterprise or activity and there is no guarantee that you will have similar results as the author as a result of reading this book.

The author reserves the right to make changes and assumes no responsibility or liability whatsoever on behalf of any purchaser or reader of these materials.

Table of Contents

Introduction

People buy from people. People want to work with people they know, like and trust.

How can I consider working with you if I can't see you? What if I can't find you online?

Social media enables people to connect. Content marketing enables people to understand one another and this quickly builds familiarity and likeability.

The more I see and hear you, the more I begin to understand you and trust you.

Over 4.9 billion people worldwide use social media on a daily basis averaging around 2 hours and 24 minutes each user every day. Billions of content are uploaded daily and the users just keep on scrolling.

Our daily lives are all linked to our shiny screens whether it's to pay for something, find a special someone through an app, talk to friends, study, work, or simply watch amusing cat videos. Either way, you're scrolling, and your customers are scrolling. Somehow you need to find each other.

What the book contains

The book contains 12 chapters that are guaranteed to change your perspective of the social media scene, bring you up to speed with the social media landscape, and provide you with practical examples and exercises to sharpen your skills.

The learning in this book is brought to you after nearly a decade of social media and financial services experience. Combining my knowledge of the financial services industry and the social media tactics I have been employing over the years.

The examples and the activities in this book have been tried and tested with mortgage brokers, financial advisers, protection advisers, and other finance professionals who have all seen excellent results and financial gains.

Every task I recommend is designed to produce income generating results in your business.

You're welcome to access the resources tab, where you'll find the exercises in the book plus additional exercises not featured in the book, at https://manukamedia.co.uk/socialmediaguide

Who is this book for?

This book aims to encourage and inspire today's UK mortgage and protection adviser or any finance professional who is in the business of people and needs to attract new customers daily. It's for the financial adviser who is too busy to tackle social media, or doesn't even know where to begin. Most financial advisers who will benefit from this book will want to increase their annual revenue, build a lifestyle business, by creating a new powerful income generating tool like social media, that hasn't worked for them before.

Is this you?

Do you feel like every other competitor of yours seems to find the courage to do video content but you don't?

Have you noticed your peers posting daily content and you have no idea how they find the time?

Have you used social media before, wasted hours of time with little to no return and feel like giving up?

By the end of this book, you should have the confidence and motivation to start developing your social media campaign, build your online presence, and create some buzzing content.

Financial advisers today struggle to use social media to their competitive advantage. Most financial advisers rely on word of mouth recommendations or existing client repeat business. This is not going to sustain your business for generations to come. Relying on existing customers will give you the next lead opportunity for as long as they stay within a 2, 3, or 5 year fixed rate mortgage. The pipeline is cyclical, and in the meantime, you need to attract new paying clients. That's if the lender doesn't swoop in there first to do a product transfer or another competitor happens to capture their attention online. The reality is, your customers hear from their lender or provider, through a diverse range of communication channels, more than they hear from you, their adviser!

Why I wrote this book

Now more than ever, consumers need a sound, personable adviser. Information on the news is confusing, and can be misleading. Many find the announcements on the news about the mortgage market quite negative and it can cause panic and despair. Hence an adviser like yourself needs to be readily available to help with educational and valuable information. Given your most precious resource is time, and you are always running out of it, the most efficient way to help your next customer is to have an abundance of content available at their fingertips.

Information is the only way. We all use the internet either for research or entertainment. Combine the two and you have yourself a social media winning recipe.

Do not threat. This book is not about turning you into a TikTok dancing machine, or a comedian. There are many styles you can adopt for your social media presence and throughout this book you will start to design your own.

The reason I bring this book to you (and I appreciate you for being here) is because my mission is to make financial services more human! I'm all about putting the personal back into personal finance and that requires people like you!

Financial advisers should be available to anyone and everyone who needs them. We need to make financial advisers more mainstream and accessible so that society can make better financial decisions which leads to a better quality of life.

My purpose is to create financial influencers and educators on social media who empower their clients and prospective clients to make sound financial decisions. Essentially, how can you become the Martin Lewis to your customers?

As an industry, financial services is aging. Many long-standing advisers have found themselves in a position of holding a strong back book of clients with nobody to pass them down to. How do we attract the next generation into this industry?

TikTok is considered the new Google. It is the search engine mostly for generation Z, Y, X. They not only enjoy themselves on TikTok for recreational purposes but they also learn about worldwide events and interests.

But how do you make your mark?

How do you stand out on social media?

The purpose of this book is to absorb the theory AND the practice as I share with you many examples and exercises that will deepen your understanding and move you forward.

How the book is structured

I've designed this book to gradually take you through a journey from mindset, understanding, through to action!

Many books often preach about the theory of why you should be doing something but not exactly HOW.

You'll be guided through a strategy building and theory learning phase, before you are exposed to tactics and common practices.

Even when new enquiries come to me and I am asked *"Hey Rosalia, can you be our social media manager and start posting for us and generate leads?"* The first step is to understand WHY. What is the goal? What is the strategy? Who is your target audience? What content ideas do you have? Do you have the relevant assets such as branding, photos, graphics, and content? I can't be your social media manager tomorrow unless we have all the above in place. It begins with the goal, the plan, and then the action.

When reading this book, you'll feel as though I am right there with you. Holding your hand and taking you through the methodical steps to putting your whole social media and content marketing campaign in place.

I will encourage you to reflect, research, think, study, and practice to ensure you don't get lost in the process.

Get ready to dive in with an open mind and a committed attitude because after all it won't work unless you work it.

Just before you dive in, a couple of caveats.

Firstly, I will be addressing trends and strategies in the book that I tried and tested with myself and clients at the time of writing this book. Trends change all the time and strategies are always adapting, therefore some might be out of date and some new ones won't even be featured in the book.

Secondly, social media moves fast and is ever changing. For example, by the time I finished writing this book the social media platform Twitter rebranded. Elon Musk now calls it X.

This means that whenever you come to read this book, try to apply it to the latest knowledge and updates of the social media scene and of course, always keep learning because social media doesn't stay still.

IF YOU DON'T BUILD A PERSONAL BRAND, SOMEONE ELSE WILL BRAND YOU WITH THE WRONG LABEL.

— Richie Norton

Chapter One: Starting Your Social Media Strategy

Social media is a powerful tool that can be used to build relationships, establish credibility, and generate leads for financial advisers. With so many social media platforms available, it can be overwhelming to choose the right one that best suits a financial adviser's goals, style, and target audience.

These are the three major keys to consider before starting your social media journey: your goal, your style, and your target audience!

Goal

Why do you want to be on social media?

What happens if you continue as you are, and do not introduce social media marketing to your existing marketing strategy?

The key here is to consider how much of a difference and impact social media can make to your business.

Will your business continue to flourish and grow in today's market, without the implementation of content marketing and social media presence?

Can you survive another 10, 20, or even 30 years in business if you are not visible online?

There are many reasons to consider implementing a social media strategy as part of your overall business and brand presence:

- Increased visibility
- Deeper credibility
- Stronger connection with existing customers
- Ability to attract new clients
- To showcase your brand
- Easily network with your peers
- Educate your audience
- Build team culture

Social media is not the only way to market your business but it is the best way to connect with a wide audience and to ensure you are accessible instantaneously with a click of a button.

According to Dataportal.com there were 66.11 million internet users in the United Kingdom in January 2023.

Needless to say, there is a lot of traffic on the internet.

Type of Media	Amount per Minute	Amount per Day
Texts sent	16 million	23.04 billion
Google searches	5.9 million	8.5 billion
Snaps shared on Snapchat	2.43 million	3.5 billion
Pieces of content shared on Facebook	1.7 million	2.45 billion

Our smartphone is the vault containing much data about our lives. It carries our images, our money, and even access to potential romantic relationships.

We've become accustomed to Amazon predicting our next purchase, having a conversation with Alexa, storing our thumbprint on our mobile phones, moving money around the world through an app, and even Netflix can predict what movies we might like to watch next, keeping us glued to the screens with minimal effort.

We're on our phones even when we're not on the phone if you get what I mean. Question is, can I see you and your brand amongst all this mobile action?

Type of Media	Amount per Minute	Amount per Day
Emails sent	231.4 million	333.22 billion
Crypto purchased	90.2 million	129.89 billion
Texts sent	16 million	24.04 billion
Google searches	5.9 million	8.5 billion
Snaps shared on Snapchat	2.43 million	3.5 billion
Pieces of content shared on Facebook	1.7 million	2.45 billion
Swipes on Tinder	1.1 million	1.58 billion
Hours streamed	1 million	1.44 billion
USD spent on Amazon	443,000	637.92 million
USD sent on Venmo	437,600	630.14 million
Tweets shared on Twitter	347,200	499.97 million
Hours spent in Zoom meetings	104,600	150.62 million
USD spent on DoorDash	76,400	110.02 million

Our phones have become the gateway to information and communication.

Are you visible on these tiny screens in multiple ways?

Email, Video, Website, Zoom, Whatsapp?

The goal on social media IS NOT just "getting leads".

Leads will absolutely be a byproduct of being present on social media. We will dive into lead generation later just in case you doubted the power of turning social media into a lead generation machine.

Perhaps your short-term goal is to make your communication channels slicker. For example, in 2020, the financial world transferred most of their communication channels from face-to-face meetings and events, to Microsoft Teams call, Zoom meetings, and webinars.

Zoom for example has existed since 2011, but for many in the financial services industry it didn't become a part of our daily practice until 2020.

Moving forward we need to be more agile and flexible when it comes to our businesses and the communication channels we provide to our customers and be open minded to embracing new technologies.

For now, when considering your goals, use the following statement to help guide you when setting your own goals and intentions:

"My goal for being on social media is to raise brand awareness, form a stronger connection with my existing clients, educate my new

potential clients, and make a difference in the world with my contribution of knowledge"

If you don't know your why, you won't be motivated enough to keep going, especially when it gets tough.

If you don't know your purpose and intention with social media, you'll put it to the bottom of the to-do list and end up resenting it.

If you don't know why, you don't have a strategy. The results will be meaningless and you'll end up wasting time and money.

Before implementing social media and content marketing, please map out your goals, your expectations, and your intentions.

Make a conscious decision about how committed you are to this plan.

Half-hearted efforts, will produce half-hearted results.

If you're diving in rather than just dipping your toe will be the between this working or not for you.

If you have decided that you are committed and ready to use social media, then let's look at the next layer of goal setting. The other aspect of goal setting is setting your expectations and intentions.

Exercise: Answer the following

1. Why social media? Why have you decided to jump in?
2. What message do you want to share on social media?
3. What's your purpose with social media?
4. Who do you want to share your message with?
5. How would you like to share your message?
6. What do you need to learn in order to be successful on social media?
7. What are your strengths and where are the gaps?
8. When do you want to start?
9. What will success look like in 3 months, 6 months, 1 year? What will good look like?
10. What is your big vision for the business and how does social media play a part?

I would also encourage you to take a screenshot of what your current profile(s) looks likes if you already have an account say with LinkedIn, Instagram Facebook etc. I recommend capturing the design of it and also some of the key numbers: number of followers, impressions, likes etc. If you know where you are currently, and where you are going, you can measure the success.

More on this when we talk about metrics and lead generation! Remember, all the exercises will be listed in the resources section via https://manukamedia.co.uk/socialmediaguide

Your style

This is the second key element we are going to discuss when it comes to planning your social media strategy.

Once you have decided on your goals, you can spend some time understanding your style.

What is your brand?

After all, in a world full of copycats, it's hard to find the realness within social media, so the best thing you can do is to be yourself.

BE YOURSELF,

EVERYONE IS ALREADY TAKEN.

– Oscar Wilde

Many think a brand is a logo, a website, and an array of colours put together to form a company.

People often confuse the real definition of a brand with logos, slogans, merchandise, and other recognizable icons.

What I believe a brand is can be summarised as follows:

A brand is a combination of experience, perception, feeling, and lasting impression somebody gets when they interact with the company's products, people, and services.

A brand is how you live and breathe your values, skills, personality, and services.

A brand is a unique experience a customer feels when they interact with that particular business.

A brand is what others say and think about who you are and what you represent.

Once you have decorated your business name by designing a cool logo, popping colours, and a catchy slogan, it's time to think deeply about your true brands' purpose.

This is how you can find your own voice and then be ready to share that on social media.

If you thought your brand was made up of logos, slogans, icons, and colours, but haven't truly found the meaning and purpose of your brand, then this exercise is for you.

If you want to truly define your brand's identity and connect with an audience who cares, then dive into this simple yet impactful exercise.

Exercise: Finding your brand with just 10 questions

1. Why does your company exist?
2. What are your company values? Pick 3 to 5 core values.
3. What are YOUR personal core values as a person not as a trading business?
4. Why do you do what you do? Why THIS business? Why THIS profession? Why did you pick this line of work?
5. What feeling would you like your customers to feel when they meet you and work with you?
6. If you were a fly (or in my case BEE) on the wall, what would you like to overhear your customers say about you to other people? Write out what you can hear them saying.
7. Why did you pick the company name you picked? What is the meaning behind this name? Why is it important to you?
8. Why did you pick the colours you picked? Even if it's grey, black, white, or purple, why were these colours important to you?
9. Which brands (outside of your industry) do you LOVE and subscribe to? Are you an Apple or Android person? Why? Are you a Starbucks or Costa kinda guy? Nike or Adidas? Waitrose or Tesco? Why?
10. List out the brands you love and WHY. Pick one phrase, feeling, or word you would use to explain why you like the brands you like.

You need to find your own style that best represents your brand, your business, and your personality.

I am here to help you find your own unique brand that means something.

There are thousands of mortgage brokers and financial advisers in the UK, so why should I pick you?

The challenge is trying to find your own style and voice whilst still playing the social media ALGORITHM game.

Whilst I don't endorse or recommend a "copy and paste" strategy or a "one-size-fits-all" approach, you do still have to play the game!

Just because dancing on TikTok was a trend, it doesn't mean you have to jump on this. However, in the spirit of the game, regardless of how uncomfortable the idea of TikTok can be, it's the place to be if you want to connect with millennials and younger generations.

It might not be your style to do video, and it might be outside of your comfort zone, BUT if you are a mortgage broker trying to attract millennials (and younger) to buy their first home for example, and your target audience likes using Instagram and TikTok, then I am here to tell you that you MUST do video.

"Video is responsible for over half (53.72%) of all global data traffic"

This is what I mean by playing the social media game.

If more than 50% of the internet traffic is video, and you want more visibility, more engagement, and more traction, then you need to be doing video whether it's your style or not!

Nobody was born a natural speaker or videographer.

These are skills you can learn. Learning comes with practice.

It doesn't mean you have to DANCE on camera, or do anything that is "not your style" because after all, as the saying goes, PEOPLE BUY FROM PEOPLE.

Your clients need you to be the best version of yourself, not someone else.

Your clients are coming to you because of YOU.

Your clients can also like and subscribe to more than one person, so be yourself as a person because the fakeness will catch you out in all the wrong ways.

So whilst I am a big advocate for "finding your own style" and doing what to you feels "on brand", you still have to play by the social media rulebook if you want it to work.

Each platform will have its own algorithm and its own preferences. Some channels prefer pictures and text, others prefer short form video content.

But how can you decide? More on this in the next chapter where we discuss the top 5 major social media platforms and how to use them, but you must understand your ideal customer first.

Knowing your ideal customer and target audience

Simply having a social media presence is not enough to be successful.

Setting yourself up with LinkedIn, Facebook, Instagram, and TikTok is not enough if you don't know your audience, how to engage with them, and what sort of content they would like to see from you.

Having an Instagram account without the strategy, is like having a 1000 business cards sitting on your desk collecting dust.

Posting random content on LinkedIn is like going to a vegan festival with a beef burger van.

You get my point.

It's not about which social media platform is most suited to financial advisers and mortgage brokers, but more about which platforms your ideal customers subscribe to.

There isn't just ONE platform that all financial advisers should use to grow their business and attract leads.

The social media platform(s) you will end up using to market your business will be determined by your ideal customer's preference.

"I don't have an ideal customer" I hear you say? *"I can help anyone and everyone".*

Back to my burger analogy.

Trying to appeal to ALL audiences gets the message confused, much like a food stand at a festival who sells "Real meat burgers" AND "Facon sausages".

Listen, I'm just as confused as you here as to why I'm jumping on this food truck analogy but we're here so go with me please.

Firstly, this creates mistrust because the product doesn't feel authentic and clear.

Secondly, it confuses the audience because the variety is too broad, and because they are confused, they do nothing and take no action.

Imagine being at the festival right now. The food court has an abundance of choice. You can see the souvlaki Greek corner, the piping hot pizza, the sizzling hot dogs, and you notice every queue is incredibly long. Every stand is packed. You try to pick one of the cuisines on offer that you love MOST. You pick the food that your taste buds are craving most.

Is it just me, or have you noticed at events that sometimes you try to make your food choice based on which is the shortest queue? But you find that they are all packed?!

Do you see how each food stand having a niche has not DECREASED the queue but instead INCREASED the influx of traffic in the queue because of their super simple menu?

This is the first thing we need to change before moving any further, and I am going to guide you through it.

From a marketing and media perspective, in a place where the internet is pushing out billions of data, standing out is becoming more and more tricky.

If you end up being generic, vague, and inconsistent, you may find that you get little to no results because it's not sticking.

Your audience needs a clear and simple message.

But who is your audience?

I am going to walk you through an exercise in order to discover who your ideal customer is and how to market your brand to them on social media.

Before we begin, I would like to add two caveats:

1. Social media trends are always changing. Your strategy will not always stay the same and it should flex around the current demands.

2. Marketing is all about trialling, testing, and tweaking. Your marketing strategy starts out as an educated guess, with plenty of research, but it will be in the implementation and results that will determine how you adapt your strategy.

   Please apply the two caveats to your own marketing strategy. It's not a case of "set and forget". You need to always revisit the plan, and adjust accordingly.

Example

Using the festival and food analogy (sorry if you are getting hungry) let's look at a simple marketing strategy and how to build one.

Let's imagine the venue of the festival is the social media platform.
The food stand/van is the vehicle in which you deliver the content and communicate with your customers.

The burger is the content. The message.

And the people in the queue are your customers, aka internet traffic, social media users.

The marketing strategy

The venue: you choose to attend a football match in London, and set up your burger van outside the entrance of the stadium.

The van: The signage on the front says "The Hatrick Burger Shack"

The content: Knowing that your audience is likely to be "meat eaters" your menu is like to have:

- A variety of burgers including cheese, and other toppings
- Buns
- Chips
- Sauces
- And beverages such as cola and beer.

The queue is made up of roaring football fans ready to bulk up before a long game. You get customers lining up early before the game AND customers stumbling out at the end of the game either hungry for more glory, or feeling the need to eat their sorrows away.

Now… if you were to provide "freshly squeezed cucumber juice" and "protein power balls" would you pitch your van up in front of a football stadium? Unlikely!

If you had a plant-based cuisine, with delicious homemade freshly squeezed juices, you are likely to choose a Yoga Festival as a potential venue to find your ideal customers.

Would you agree?

After seeing the example above, how can we apply this to the financial world?

First, let me take you through the exercise you need to complete in order to get clear on your customer avatar.

A customer avatar, also known as a buyer persona or marketing persona, is a fictional representation of your ideal customer. It is a detailed description of the characteristics, behaviours, and preferences of your target audience, based on data and research.

Creating a customer avatar is a useful tool for businesses to better understand their target audience and create more effective marketing strategies. By having a clear picture of who their ideal customer is, businesses can tailor their messaging and content to better resonate with them, and ultimately increase their chances of converting them into paying customers.

Exercise: Getting to know your ideal customer.

If you have 50, 100, or more customers, then you definitely have enough data to be able to do this exercise quite quickly.

If you have fewer customers than 50, or you're just starting out in your business, then this exercise will still be useful to make a hypothesis about the audience you might like to target.

Either way, this exercise will help you have a clearer picture of your ideal customer in mind.

Give your ideal customer a name. Pick a customer who you would LOVE to see many more like them in your business.

Find out as much as you can about that perfect client including the following features:

- Location
- Profession
- Age

- Relationship status
- Family life
- Income
- Hobbies
- Networks, groups
- Preferred social media channel
- Their beliefs and values. Are they sporty? Do they truly care about world events? Do they care for the environment?
- Home style
- Goals and aspirations
- Why did they come to you?
- How did they find you?
- What was their challenge?
- What problem did they come to you with?
- What would they say about you?
- What feedback did they give you?
- What questions did they ask?

Get to know your customer not only as a client but as a friend. Who are they as people?

Getting to know what your customer's pains, gains, and goals are, really helps you to do two things and therefore elevate you as an advisor:

1) Helps you understand them so much better that in turn you're able to deliver better customer outcomes

2) Helps you to form a better bond with them and build a stronger relationship.

Knowing your ideal customer doesn't just help you attract NEW business, but it aids retention too!

Earlier, I said that I would build a very simple marketing plan for a financial adviser that was similar to the food truck but specific to a potential mortgage client.

Example of a Customer Avatar

Here is an example which I went through with a client (anonymous) and would like to show you the findings from our research.

Data from an existing ideal client

- 33 years old
- Mainly uses Instagram and Facebook with friends and family, travel inspiration, and sports
- Uses LinkedIn for business, and to connect with clients.
- Renting in Essex
- Introduced to mortgage broker by your tennis buddy and client at the local leisure centre
- Andy also plays tennis.
- Andy is self-employed web developer
- Has had a few jobs in the past
- No children

- Working in London and commutes
- Wants to buy a home with girlfriend
- Clean credit
- Andy is very green conscious. He is concerned about climate change
- Travels a lot. Does hikes, and adventurous sports

The marketing strategy

The venue: tennis club in Essex

The van: I suggest to the mortgage broker to sponsor a networking breakfast meeting at the tennis club for members. The original client who introduced the mortgage broker to Andy, and Andy themselves, agree to attend the event and even invite a few more of their buddies.

I implement for the broker, an email marketing service via the club to promote the event, and also join the Facebook members group to discuss the upcoming event, connect with delegates, and share content.

The content: Knowing that the audience is likely to be into sports, health, fitness, and also in Essex, we decide to deliver content about the following:

- Getting on the property ladder. How to stop renting and start owning your own place
- Taking care of your health. Protecting your health and income

- Saving and investing for the future
- Tax efficiency and regulations for the self employed
- And finally: green mortgages and ethical investing.

The mortgage broker, after a little bit of pushback, accepted my invitation to go live on Facebook during the talk for anybody who wasn't able to attend in person and then later over the next few days we posted bitesize pieces of information on social media taken from the event.

The people in the room are not all going to be exactly like Andy, but we know that a good place to start could be the tennis club because we already have an existing client there who has now referred the broker to another!

The pattern starts to emerge and whilst these two customers came to the broker "by accident" you can actually capitalise on it and make it more of a proactive strategy to see if you can expand your reach within this network.

Combining the face to face engagement, with the email marketing, and Facebook communication channels, will create the perfect buzz around your brand and engage the right audience.

This is the perfect balance of being seen in multiple locations both online and in person.

You have a split between events, email, and social media.

How can you apply this simple example to your own customer avatar?

You can download your copy of the "Buyer Persona" worksheet in the bonus resources section at https://manukamedia.co.uk/socialmediaguide

Chapter Two: Becoming Visible

People want to do business with those they know, like, and trust.

KNOW, LIKE, & TRUST.

If I can't see you, how can I trust you?

This is where I introduce you to a powerful formula that is crucial to your success on social media.

Have you heard of the 4-11-7 rule?

Research by Google suggests that a buyer needs 7 hours of interaction, across 11 touch points, in 4 separate locations before they make a purchase.

That's 7 hours of content. 11 multiple ways to communicate. Across 4 channels.

Ask yourself: do you have 7 or more hours of binge worthy content about you and your services?

If I were to Google you today, what will I find about you?

Inevitably, whether it's a warm referral or a brand-new customer, they are going to look you up on Google!

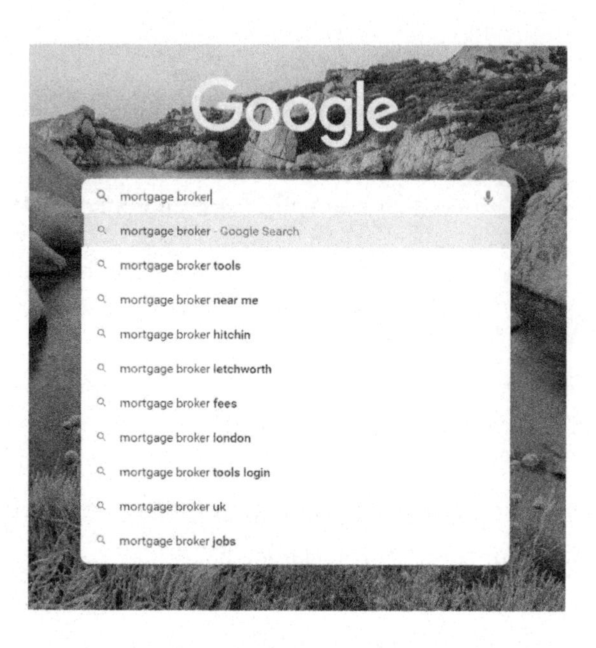

Did you know that 99% of the time if someone were to Google your name, the first or second link in the search results on Google is your LinkedIn profile?

It is more than likely that if a client were to research for example "John Smith mortgage broker" on Google, your LinkedIn would be their first impression of you as a person and brand.

It's the first social media page that ranks high up on Google, so would it be fair to say that as a minimum you need a standout LinkedIn profile as well as a reputable website?

If you want to be a recognisable brand and be front of mind with your customers, then here's the formula I am going to teach you.

The 4 - 11 - 7 formula

The goal is: more touchpoints = more visibility with clients = more trust = more leads!

Let's start with the number 4. Four Channels.

The more recognisable you are, the more they trust you.

Which 4 channels are you currently using right now to connect with your customers?

Which 4 locations may I be able to find you and your business?

The aim is to make it super easy for your customers to find you, identify you, and connect with you.

Channels include: website, social media, email, phone, text, book, online webinar, mail, radio, TV, and many other.

Right now, if all you have is phone and email, you're decreasing your chances of being connected to your customer by 50%.

Double your chances, by increasing the number of channels you are visible on.

Remember, just having a Facebook and LinkedIn profile doesn't cut it. It's not going to tick the box.

The social media profiles you have need to be active, optimised, engaging, and seen by the right people!

Exercise: Picking your 4 communication channels

Don't guess.

Marketing is indeed about trial and error, testing, and tweaking. But not guessing!

Ask your clients!

Ask your top 10 favourite clients of all time to feedback to you. Ask them the following 8 simple questions:

1. How do you best like to communicate with me?
2. What communication channel am I missing that you would appreciate?
3. Which communication channel did you find most annoying or would prefer not having?
4. Which is your favourite social media platform where you would enjoy staying in touch with me and learning from me too?
5. On a scale of 1 to 10 how helpful was my website in providing you the right information needed?
6. On a scale of 1 to 10 how helpful and informative is my XYZ social media channel?
7. Do you enjoy reading newsletters and find them helpful?
8. Do you prefer phone, email, text, social media, or face to face?

Now let's break down the number 11. Eleven touch points.

On average it takes seven to eight touchpoints to close a sale.

Getting a mortgage is not like getting a new pair of trainers.

We don't need a mortgage every day, and the buying cycle is much longer in comparison to buying an everyday low-cost commodity.

A mortgage is a once in a lifetime experience that not everybody has the privilege of attaining.

Just over 4.4 million households live in the private rented sector in England, 19% of all households. By comparison, 17% (4.0 million) live in the social rented sector and 65% (15.4 million) are owner occupiers.

Therefore, when "advertising" on social media, be mindful that your viewers may not be ready to buy right away.

The key is to help them be more aware of you, without feeling like you are trying to sell to them at every opportunity.

You don't want to be Ms Spammy McSpammy.

The reason I said "advertising" is because that's probably what you or your colleagues have been doing, right?

"100% mortgages are back, call me right away"

"Do you need to refinance? Don't go to your bank, I can do it!"

"Has another broker let you down? You should have come to me!"
"Rates are going up, why haven't you called me yet?"

The best policy on social media when it comes to mortgages and general finance talk such as, pensions, investments, insurance, and savings, is: **education and value over selling, always.**

The audience just needs to know:

1) Do I know about you?
2) Do I like you? And
3) Do I trust you?

THEY will make the call on whether or not to reach out to you based on how confident they are on the three questions above. That's why you need to make it easier for them during the consideration phase of the buying cycle by increasing the number of interactions they have with you and your brand.

The more they see you, the sooner they will start knowing, liking, and trusting you.

A customer might view your website once?

They might take one or two phone calls, but then will opt to continue all communications via WhatsApp or email.

But I guarantee you, they are scrolling on social media DAILY!

Exercise: How are you communicating with your customer?

Have a look at your latest 12 completions. Let's do a test with 12 of your latest customers.

How many times did you communicate with each customer? Work out the average across the 12 you are testing this on.

What communication channels did you use? List all the ones you used.

Email
Whatsapp
Facebook
Newsletter
Phone call
Website visit
Letter in the post

Where did your customer see you?

TV
Google ad
Podcast guest
Networking event
Featured in the press
TikTok video or a Reel on Instagram
Connection request on LinkedIn / Facebook

And finally, the number 7, which stands for seven hours of content.

"How on earth am I going to produce 7 hours of content???"

If you are thinking this, please stop panicking.

I want to show you that it's easier than you might actually think!

First things first, let's do a quick audit to see where you are, and where you need to be.

Exercise: Google yourself.

Yes. Google your name, your company name, and make a list of all the resources and links that show up on the first page.

Are you featured in the press?
Do you have helpful resources and downloadables on your website?
Do you have social media videos?
Have you been a guest on a podcast?
Have you released a white paper?

Secondly, once you have done the audit above, know that content is not built all in one go.

It's not a set and forget procedure.

Just because you have been on one podcast as a guest, does not mean you now forget about it and not do any more.

Just because you've written one paper does not mean you leave it on the internet to collect dust.

Content is ongoing.

Content is communication.

Keep the communication active.

Keep creating content daily!

The Lifespan of Social Media Posts

Twitter	15 Minutes
Tiktok	30 Minutes
Facebook	6 Hours
LinkedIn	24 Hours
Instagram	48 Hours
Youtube	20+ Days
Pinterest	4 Months
Blog Post	1 Year or More

And that is why!

The lifespan of your content on social media, that is the length of time in which people engage with your social media content, is as you can see very short!

That's why you don't just create the content ONCE and forget about it.

Instead, see content as your ongoing communication method with your client.

Content stops = communication stops.

As the saying goes… Out of sight out of mind.

Chapter Three: Which Social Media Platform Should I Be Using?

I think it's safe to say we all agree on using social media to increase our brand awareness and visibility, correct?

I've also mentioned that you need to be present where your customers are likely to be.

Chances are, today, most of us use ALL the platforms at some point or another, so in this chapter you will find out how to optimise your social media strategy using the top 5 major social media platforms of this current time.

Most of us have a Facebook profile and a LinkedIn profile.

Many, even those who don't like to admit it, downloaded TikTok during 2020 and have been secretly or publicly addicted to this short video content platform.

But which one SHOULD you have?

The first answer to this question is decided by, you guessed it, your client. When doing your buyer persona, and research with your clients, which platform was the most popular?

The second way to answer that question is - which platform do YOU use the most, are most familiar with, and ... have the most connections on?

P.S. If you are a mortgage broker and you have 2,000 mortgage broker connections on LinkedIn it is pointless. Being connected to hundreds, or thousands of your competitors won't bring in business.

The third layer to answering this question is: Which platforms are the most popular?

Favourite Social Media Platforms as of April 2023

Percentage of active social media users aged 16 to 64 who say that each option is their "favourite" social media platform.

WhatsApp	16.6%
Instagram	14.7%
Facebook	13.7%
WeChat	13.6%
Tiktok	6.1%
Douyin	5.9%
Twitter	3.5%
FB Messenger	2.4%
Telegram	2.2%
Line	1.9%
Kuaishou	1.7%
Pinterest	1.5%
Snapchat	1.3%
QQ	1.1%
iMessage	0.9%
Xiaohongshu	0.9%

I will caveat this with the date, as this is data based on the recent stats taken in April 2023 by wearesocial.

This means that trends can change and even new platforms can come into the market or exit.

Clubhouse who?

Clubhouse app launched as an audio-based social media platform that used to be an invite-only iOS app. Its usage peaked around March 2021 but has since then lost more than 80% of users. The name subsequently changed to Shortcut but as you guessed it, nobody actually really talks about it.

On that note, notice how Clubhouse and TikTok emerged at similar times, but only TikTok truly stuck it out and still creates buzz around the app.

Some jumped into Clubhouse. Others boarded the TikTok train.

It was a 50/50 gamble.

Who could have predicted which one would really have taken off?

A wise choice would have been to do BOTH. But "who has the time?" I hear you say.

This is why marketing is trial and error. It's testing your hypothesis, executing the tasks, and then checking the results.

You'll notice that WhatsApp is a social media platform even though we see it as a simple messaging tool but the most frequently shared content on WhatsApp are: gifs, images, voice notes, and videos.

WhatsApp has also added the "My status" feature copying the "Story" of Instagram, TikTok, and Facebook, in order to encourage contacts to engage with one another.

LinkedIn tried to adopt the story feature, and after a few months, took it down as it wasn't adopted on this platform as much as it was on others.

Did I try it?

Absolutely.

When the story feature came out on LinkedIn I used it multiple times per day. I enjoyed it but it lacked the design element that Instagram for example does well.

I even got business from it, but in the grand scheme of things, LinkedIn wasn't satisfied with the overall take up so decided to take it down.

Even as marketers we try things and it doesn't always work.

This is why it's a social media game.

We play with the functionality of the platform. Some work. Some don't. I know it's difficult to stay motivated and to be patient with it, but stay agile. Have fun with it and test it.

Other than Whatsapp, which we can safely keep as our instant messaging channel, the next top two true social media channels are Instagram and Facebook.

For a long time, Instagram and Facebook have been battling for the top spot and I have seen them switch around a few times.

With the latest new feature on Instagram being Reels, a subsequent novelty following the success of TikTok, Instagram kicks Facebook off the top spot.

Facebook responded by ALSO introducing the Reels feature to their platform but it still doesn't quite match up to Instagram. Having said all this, I have to point out the obvious that although Instagram, Whatsapp, and Facebook behave differently, they are actually all owned by one company. Meta.

However, it goes back to the point of your ideal customer. If your ideal customer loves LinkedIn and this is where they hang out, then it doesn't matter if LinkedIn is in the top spot or the 10th spot, you should be on it!

Being present on the major platforms is essential for visibility and connectivity. Being visible across multiple platforms allows us to cast our net wide and show different elements of our brand in creative ways.

Having a multichannel presence enables us to build further trust with our audience.

This cross-channel platform way of marketing increases recognition!

The more you're seen, the more memorable you become.

As the saying goes "out of sight out of mind", hence the power of the 4-11-7 rule.

Chapter Four: How To Use The Top 5 Trending Platforms

Let's discover how best to use the current major 5 social media platforms based on TODAY'S trends.

"A recent study analysing Facebook age demographics shows that the age group with the highest number of Facebook users is 25 to 34. 30% of all active Facebook users fall within this range, which totals 596.8 million people. This is followed by the 18-to-24 age group, which makes up 21.5% of all Facebook users worldwide."

It's safe to assume that most people you meet, have Facebook! But does your ideal customer have it and USE it?

"According to the breakdown of Facebook users by age group, the social network isn't frequented as much by the older generation. 55- to 64-year-olds make up just 7.2% of Facebook's total user base, while those aged 65 and above represent just 5.6%."

The way I see Facebook is that it's a friends and family engagement tool, but there is still plenty of business to be done!

Despite there only being 7.2% of users within the 55 to 64 age bracket, we're actually always running successful Facebook ad campaigns for several independent financial advisers targeting people approaching retirement age for example.

Check out these stats for a client of ours and what we managed to achieve within 14 days of going live:

- 48,527 impressions
- 791 clicks to the landing page we built
- £0.29 cost per click
- 3 meetings
- 2 customers converted and the client made back more than his investment!!

The campaign consisted of:

- 1 filming day to shoot the content
- 2 live video ads were used which we recorded and edited
- 2 picture ads with copy which we wrote (and we also took the pictures on the filming day)
- All 4 pieces of content ran at the same time to gauge the interest levels

Within the first week we instantly saw 60% of the traffic going to video number 2 so we stopped the other video and focused on the top performing one.

Yes. Of all 4 pieces of content, the 2 videos were the ones that generated more than 60% of the traffic to the landing page.

Sharing this is to show you that with the right content and copy you can totally speak to your ideal customer effectively even if the stats appear to be low.

Chances are, you've had a Facebook account since you were at school, university, or got it later in life when wanting to stay connected to family and friends.

That's why when a stranger sends you a "Friend" request, you think "creeeeep".

We get uncomfortable when people we don't know send us a friend request.

Conversely, when a stranger on LinkedIn sends us a request we think *"Ding! New business opportunity?"* orrrr… you might be thinking *"Doh! More spam and pushy sales incoming?"*

More on this later….

Ultimately, Facebook is a hub for where friends and family connections live. Where you get reminders of people's birthdays, and you get to see how your friend's children are growing up so fast. Not to mention, you get to see what your cousin ate for dinner last night.

So if this is your overall experience of Facebook, you've been doing it absolutely right!

However… you are missing a trick!

You're probably thinking that because Facebook is an endless stream of baby, pet, and food posts, that you can't possibly do business or mortgage talk on there.

You can indeed!

Think about it… Facebook is most likely to be the platform where you have the most connections, the WARMEST connections of people who already love and care about you, and it's the platform where you probably have the most diverse range of connections, from friends, to family, to ex colleagues, and clients?

The power of Facebook is underestimated especially if you are in the B2C business.

As a mortgage broker, financial adviser, accountant, make-up artist, gardener, plumber, hairdresser, and wedding photographer, Facebook is a great place to grow your business!

Facebook is home to networking, community groups, and recommendation groups too!

Try this:

Using the Groups search bar within Facebook:

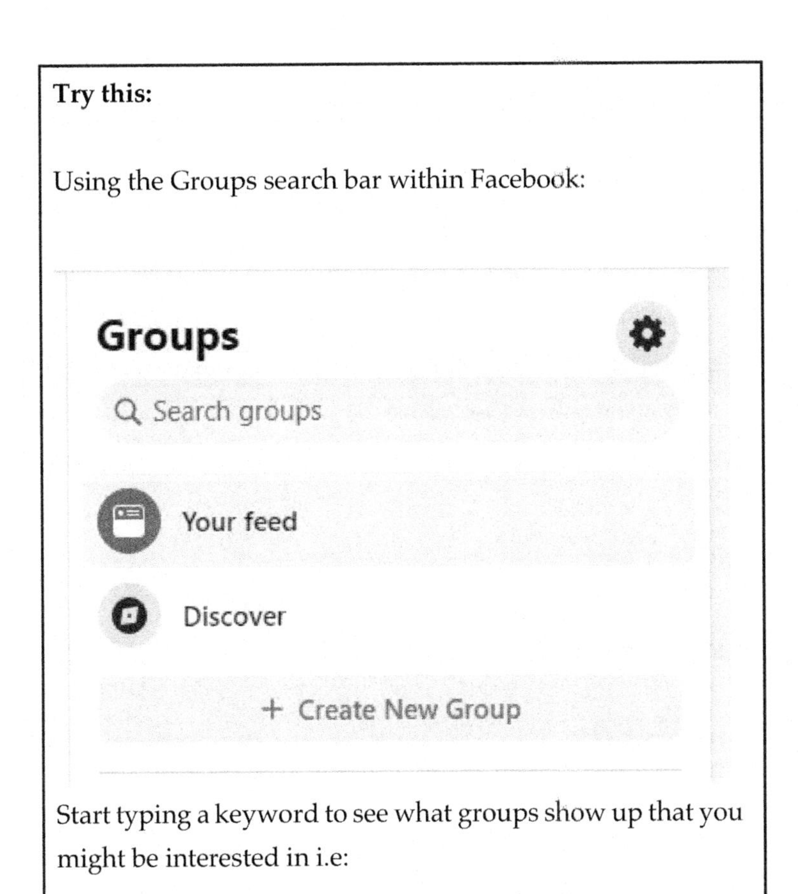

Start typing a keyword to see what groups show up that you might be interested in i.e:

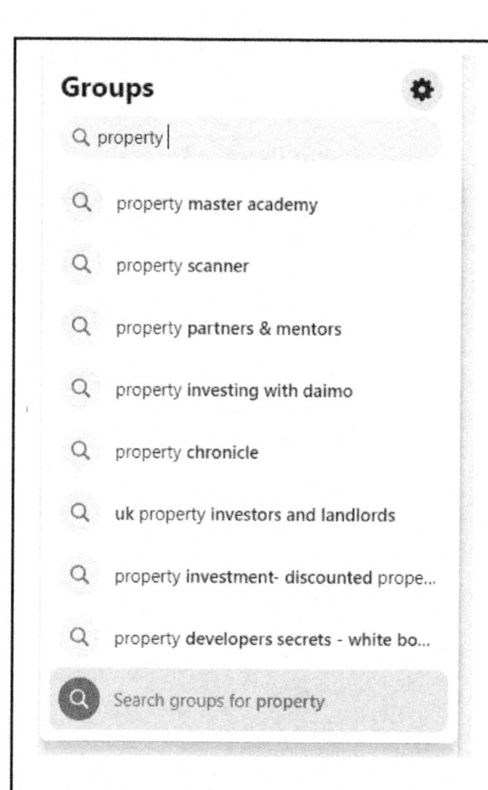

The key word here being property, as an example, you can see the suggested searches Facebook is trying to help you out with.

You can get MORE specific by typing in a geographic location i.e:

Through this search functionality, you can find likeminded people.

If you are a mortgage broker then it might be worth mingling and networking with property aficionados because guess what, they'll need loans and mortgages!

By knowing your ideal customer, you can start to make clear and specific searches on social media to find more of your ideal customers.

For example, a financial adviser I have been working with, has realised that her brand is all about "Empowering mums to take control of their finances and not rely on a man to deal with the money at home". So based on this powerful and clear mission, we did some research on Facebook and found some interesting groups:

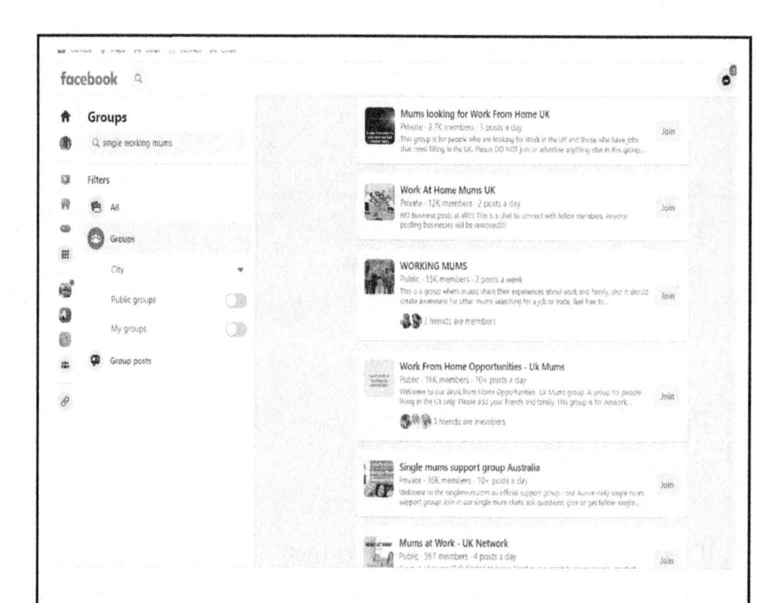

My client's mission is to meet and greet with as many of the group members as possible. She provides powerful content to support the members of the groups she has joined. She doesn't pitch or sell in these groups. She shares helpful hints, tips, motivation, and information.

Now you try.

See which key words, associated with your ideal customer, have a group that might be relevant on Facebook.

Be sure to check out the rules of that Facebook group and then try to be as social, helpful, and available as possible.

This is the online version of networking!

P.S. if a group doesn't exist. Make one!

Facebook is a great place to grow a community. If you think that your town is in desperate need of a Property networking group or a "Working mums" networking event, then host one!

Being a host of a group or event gives you instant credibility. Being a leader of a group means people come to you first! You are their source of knowledge.

When the door doesn't exist, build one ...

As we all know, word of mouth referrals for a financial adviser are the lifeblood of their business.

We know that referrals are the strongest form of lead, right?

What do you think Facebook is?

Facebook is the digital version of word of mouth!

It's a public way for the masses to see what is being liked, trusted, and recommended.

Example 1: Susan posts a picture of her newly groomed garden with her dog playing under the tree and says this: *"Thank you to @Gary Green Fingers who has transformed our beautiful garden into this little haven. Fab job, cheers Gazza".* Now Susan, friends of Susan, and friends of friends of Susan can now see Gary! Gary received many compliments on Susan's posts and quickly starts to notice friend requests and direct messages requesting a quote
Example 2: Ben posts on Facebook saying: "Does anybody know a good local gardener please?" Susan spots this, and remembers her beautifully manicured garden and decides to be a decent human being and tags Gary Green Fingers, with a glowing recommendation. Gary notices this and quickly engages with Ben, as well as offering his thanks to Susan.
Example 3: Gary Green Fingers is super chuffed with his latest landscaping project at Susan's that he takes a few pictures of his before and after transformation. He posts about it on Facebook, tagging his client Susan. Susan showers Gary with compliments by commenting on his post (which opens up the visibility of Gary's post to Susan's network, and presto!)

That is the power of word of mouth - di.gi.ta.lly!

If you want to increase referrals thick and fast in your business, get your friends, family, and clients to rave about you!

There's nothing better than other people talking about your brand.

As you can see from example number 3, Gary has taken responsibility to raise awareness around his work. He doesn't just rely on Susan. He wants to promote his business by telling the story.

Are you harnessing the power of Facebook and the power of connections?

Invite your clients like Susan, to share their good news stories, but also remember to be like Gary and take responsibility for the brand awareness of your business.

After all, it starts and ends with you.

I always say: Facts Tell Stories sell!

And this quote could not be more perfect for a platform like Instagram.

Instagram is a very visual app.

The style of the original Instagram was all about your beautifully curated life summed up on a grid.

A catalogue of the "Instagram Life". The yacht. The perfect face contour. The dream partner. The dream beach bod.

You get the picture…

The purpose of Instagram was to share perfectly curated moments in just one little square.

However, now more than ever before, the REAL people of Instagram are taking over.

It's all about the real talk. The candid pictures. Behind the scenes. The progress pictures. The vulnerability chats. Real people on Instagram are here to stay, making the platform more popular than ever before.

It's not just about celebrities anymore, but about world events, political campaigns, environmental protests, and real people building a life for themselves.

This is absolutely the place for you.

This is absolutely a place where you can build a business, connect with your community, and sell your products.

Yes, there's an Instagram shop, like Facebook Marketplace, where brands such as Ted Baker, Zara, Ocado, and Dyson are selling their products.

But there is plenty of money talk too!

Instagram is a place where you'll find property developers documenting their property transformations, as well as the crypto and bitcoin "gurus".

"48.2% of all Instagram users are female while 51.8% are male. 31.7% of Instagram users are 25-34 years old. 30.2% of Instagram users are 18-24 years old. 2.1% of Instagram users are 65+ years old."

The winning content on Instagram is by those who humanise their content, and make their offering approachable.

It's a great way to share your brand's narrative, and allow existing clients as well as potential new customers to experience your brand in a fun way.

As I mentioned before, people want to work with people they KNOW, LIKE and TRUST.

Engaging short form content on Instagram such as Reels, Stories, and Pictures, is a great way to visually share your brand's story and allow your audience to enjoy the experience.

Learning from the iconic brands such as Lego, we can take away how even the biggest brands who are well known, still simplify their message and make it super relatable and approachable for the general public.

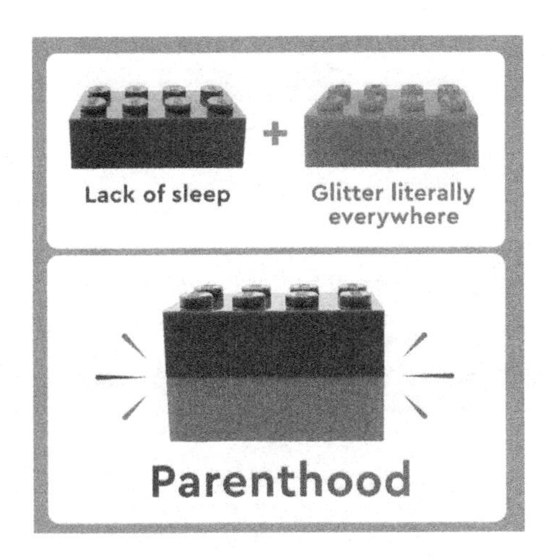

The famous saying sticks:

"KISS: Keep It Simple Stupid."

Try this: Research some of your favourite brands on Instagram.

Follow them and check out their content.

Make a conscious effort of looking at these brands now as if you were a marketer.

What is their messaging like? How do they play with their message? How do they tell a story and connect with the audience?

Marketing campaigns don't need to be grand, expensive, elaborate, or complicated.

It's a simple idea. A story. And consistency!

Try out some fun and engaging messages on Instagram and see what works for your ideal customer.

Business content for humans.

"You can't post that! This is not Facebook. This is a professional platform!" said the self-appointed LinkedIn Police.

Yawn.

LinkedIn is where PEOPLE, BUSINESS, STUDENTS, POLITICIANS, LEADERS and INFLUENCERS unite.

Yes, in 2002 when LinkedIn was launched, it started out as a CV platform. A business platform where employers and employees could find each other.

As LinkedIn started to become profitable by 2007, people and businesses also started to capitalise on this networking platform.

Content in the early days was very much about features and benefits, ads, sales tactics, job adverts, and company news stories.

Today we have a variety of content flooding our screens on LinkedIn. From Richard Branson playing chess...

Fun chess battle with Sam.

To the latest developments by Cancer Research UK.

+ Follow

Breakthrough! Scientists we fund at The Francis Crick Institute and UCL have found vital early clues from lung cancer cells, which indicate where and when they might spread to next in the body - part of the nine-year TRACERx study.

Professor Charles Swanton, TRACERx lead researcher and our chief clinician, said: "TRACERx recognises that cancer isn't static, and the way we treat patients shouldn't be either."

Read more about the findings of this landmark study, and what they mean for people affected by cancer in future: https://cruk.ink/3KTWOni

#TRACERx #LungCancer #CancerResearch

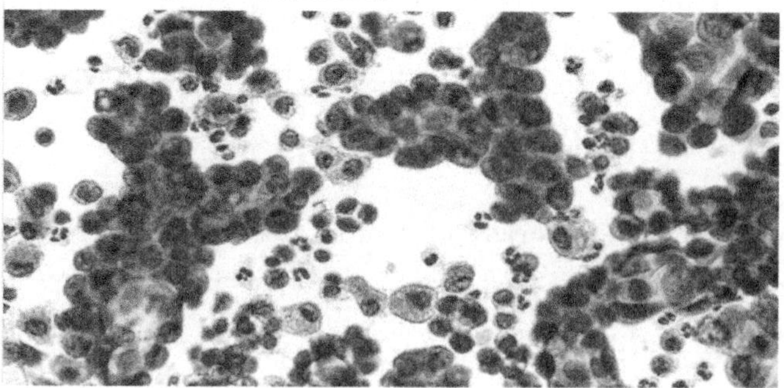

Why?

Because "business people" are human.

Companies are run by humans.

Humans work for companies.

Humans use products.

We feel better when we're connected. Happiness is connection. We certainly learnt about the power of connection, or the lack of it, back in 2020.

LinkedIn is a great place to share your story, your company's mission, the hobbies and interests you partake in, and the world events going on around you, because after all, that is what makes you YOU.

LinkedIn is open to content that connects people, and shares ideas.

Just like any other platform, LinkedIn users are human therefore humanising your content and making it relatable totally works.

Many people disagree with this.

This is because they want to keep LinkedIn as "the place to do business".

Business is done where people meet. That's it.

You can do business with someone at a birthday party if you really wanted to and the need arises.

You can do business on the beach, aeroplane, or in the gym.

I have met my ideal clients at the gym, at a salsa dance class, at a motivational speaking event, at my friend's house, at a networking event, on a plane, and in a restaurant.

I strike up conversations with people. We make a connection. And then guess what ....

THEY ADD ME ON SOCIAL MEDIA!

Once the face to face conversation seems to be drawing to an end, and the person wants to continue staying in touch, what do they ask for?

"Are you on social media?"

"What's your number?"

Those are the two most frequently asked questions.

When people want to stay in touch they exchange numbers AND their social media profiles.

This is because it's a personable way to stay up to date with what you are doing.

This is why LinkedIn is the perfect place to stay REAL and human.

Use LinkedIn as a way for your audience to get to know you to a point where they actually see themselves doing business with you.

Do you ever feel like you're always late to the party?

Or you find yourself saying *"They got there first that's why they are successful"*.

That's the fresh new opportunity on the social media scene we were given with TikTok back in 2020.

Some took it.

Some watched.

Some are now catching up.

At a glance, you'd be right in thinking it was an entertainment app for Gen Z who spent all day doing memes, dance routines, and funny cat videos.

But how is it now a lead generation machine for the few advisers who did latch on and make a success of it?

If you blinked and missed it, I am here to tell you that yes, it is an effective lead generation tool for many already successful mortgage advisers on the scene.

From the States, to the UK, Poland, and Australia, there are many financial advisers on the platform from all over the world sharing financial top tips, market updates, case studies, and answers to questions other users pose.

Notice how I didn't say "advice"...

Advice would be against financial promotions and against the FCA guidelines, so advisers have cleverly designed their marketing around guidance, examples, helpful resources, education, and entertainment.

Same goes for any other platform. Be it Facebook, Instagram, LinkedIn, or TikTok, you do not want to be posting advice.

Whilst there is a lot of comedy on TikTok, there is still a place for the money talk.

Here are some numbers for you to demonstrate just how popular money, investments, and property content is on TikTok.

There are the top 12 trending hashtags with either millions or BILLIONS of views.

1. #money with 122.1B views
2. #property with 4.2B views
3. #mortgage with 2.2B views
4. #investing with 12.2B views
5. #financegoals 28.4M views

6. #financialfreedom 5.5B views
7. #success 32.1Bviews
8. #trading 21.2B views
9. #financecoach 23.4M views
10. #stocks 9.0B views
11. #motivation 77.4B views
12. #finances 482.9M views

"TikTok gained 1.36 billion downloads (45% of total downloads) from Q1 in 2020 through to Q2 in 2021. TikTok currently has 1 billion monthly active users worldwide."

As of April 2023, research shows that the platform is still very much popular amongst the younger generations.

'Ages 10-19 are 25% of users. Ages 20-29 are 22.4% of users. Ages 30-39 is 21.7% of users. Ages 40-49 is 20.3% of users.'

But what does this generation want and why should you be talking to them?

Below is an example of what this generation may want to see from you. If you are looking to target millennials, generation Y and Z, then I have a 20-day hack for you that you can start to implement right away!

Try this

20 in 20 days challenge

Try these super engaging and simple to create posts that you can film right away.

Top tip: the more natural you are the better. You do not need a super professional setup to get going.

1. A day in the life
2. Go With Educational Videos
3. Share a Quick Tip
4. Try Q/A Videos
5. Spread Words of Positivity
6. Talk About the Current Happenings
7. Use Trending Sound Clip with a video or picture of you working
8. Reveal a Life Hack
9. Test the Viral Hack
10. Behind the Scene Videos
11. Give a tour of your workplace
12. Funny pet video
13. Give a short tutorial
14. Try lip syncing to a trending audio
15. Post about your favourite books/movies/hobbies
16. Try a duet with another professional in your industry
17. Share a top tip

18. Try a tending challenge i.e recording your reaction to a clip you've seen
19. Share inspiration i.e home inspiration, travel destinations, business ideas
20. Client news, testimonials, and reviews

TikTok, as well as other channels we have already talked about, will enable you to educate the next buyer.

These social media platforms are giving you access to the next wave of home buyers.

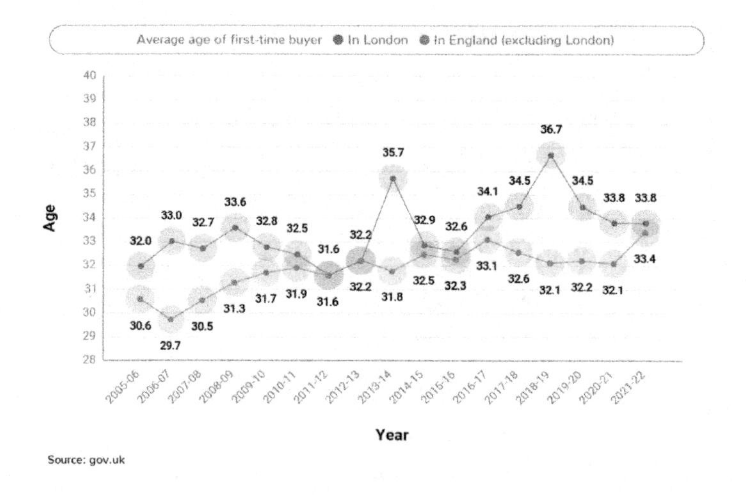

Source: gov.uk

"The average age of a first-time buyer in the UK has been steadily creeping up over the years. As of 2021-22, the average first-time buyer outside London is 33.4."

With the rise in the cost of living, the mortgage rate spikes, and the increase of house prices in the UK, these circumstances have been making it considerably harder for potential buyers to save up a deposit and buy their first home.

This is where you come into it.

The next generation of home buyers are struggling enough as it is and therefore need a trustworthy source of information to navigate the difficult world of property.

When they are scrolling through social between, between one cat video and the next, there will be some educational videos in the mix that they will stop and listen to.

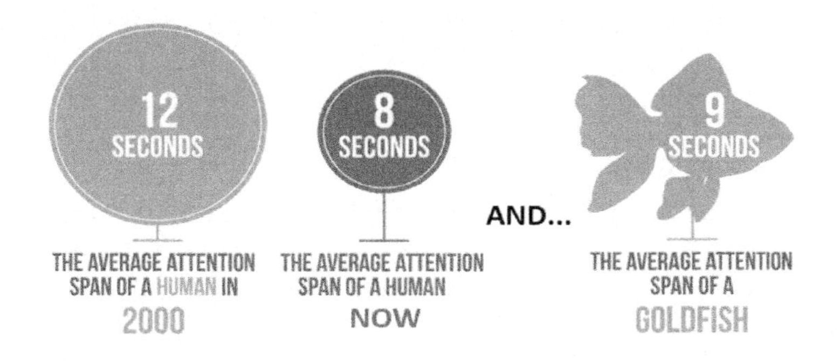

The reasons TikTok works well for new home buyers to absorb information and take an interest is because it's short.

The information can be delivered with speed, hence grabbing their attention and peaking their interest.

But don't be fooled...

Having a short attention span and comparing it to a Goldfish is not an insult.

It's not a bad thing.

Today, millennials to Gen Z are fast thinkers, quick decision makers, and generally very good at multitasking.

That's why, platforms such as Instagram, TikTok, and now even YouTube, have prioritised short form content such as stories, Reels, Shorts, and TikToks.

The information can easily be absorbed in a matter of seconds, and if the viewer is interested enough, I promise you they'll binge your content.

Although videos on TikTok range between 15 seconds to maximum 3 minutes, users spend on average 45 minutes to an hour on the platform.

All those mini 20 second videos add up.

Within the hour, I can learn how to paint by numbers, contour my face, learn a DIY hack, curl my hair, and save a deposit for my first home.

This is what is appealing to the users of TikTok.

They can learn a lot in a short space of time.

There are no signs of YouTube slowing down. With over 2.1 billion users, YouTube continues to be the best video streaming, and video content making platform. YouTube sees approximately 122 million users per day.

"In fact, YouTube is so dominant in online video sharing and video content creation that 78.8% of video marketers believe YouTube is the most effective platform for marketing."

YouTube has been around now for 18 years versus Instagram which has been around for 13.

Whilst YouTube has been one of the longest standing social media platforms, particularly for video streaming and long form video content, it has had to rapidly adapt to today's demands of short form content.

Enter, Shorts.

YouTube Shorts came out in September 2020, a month after Instagram Reels.

TikTok was already in the lead at this point, so YouTube and Instagram were only following suit.

This platform is very diverse where you'll find a wide variety of content ranging from gamers, to chefs, to make up tutorials, music videos, and life changing events.

YouTube allows viewers to watch the news, learn about life events, watch their favourite artists, and even learn a new skill.

This is the place to be if you want to educate your audience on life changing events such as buying a home, saving a deposit, investing money, and planning for a healthy retirement.

The world of financial services is so deep and complex that it would be handy to have more educators, like yourself, on this FREE app.

On that note, I will take this opportunity to make a point that I think I have missed because I took it for granted.
THESE SOCIAL MEDIA PLATFORMS (at least at the point of writing this book) ARE FREE.

You get to connect with your friends, family, and clients for FREE.

YouTube, despite there being a lot of ads, allows you to post content for free. Some even get paid!

"To start earning money directly through YouTube, you must have at least 1,000 subscribers and 4,000 watch hours in the past year, or

1,000 subscribers with 10 million valid public Shorts views within the past 90 days. Once you reach either of those, you can apply to YouTube's Partner Program and monetize your channel."

Estimated Total Earnings by Channel

Number of Total Subscribers	913,000 Subscribers
Number of Total Video Views	91 Million
Total Estimated Earnings	$259,304
Average Earnings Per Video	$979

So let's get this straight ..

You get to use the app for free? Yes.

But actually, you can get paid by YouTube to post content?

Yes

What is there not to like?

I'll be honest with you.

I didn't start out in my business with a YouTube strategy.

I did not start out with all the big 5.

I started with LinkedIn primarily, and then Instagram, and lastly Facebook.

This is because, my ideal customers were mainly on LinkedIn.

As you know from my foreword, I started my business during a pandemic after being made redundant. I had to start quickly, and scale fast. Without any savings put aside for an event like this, and my redundancy money only lasting me till Christmas, I had to find some clients quickly therefore my strategy needed to be small and super focused, rather than broad and wide.

I spent A LOT of time on LinkedIn and 3 years later, after 11,000 plus connections, I am able to spend more time to build other channels.

I am now on all the big 5 and Spotify too.

Actually, I am now also on Amazon with this book!

I mention this because I want to show you that:

a) You can absolutely build a business from scratch with no experience and no clients just by simply using social media.

b) You don't need to be famous to be successful through social media

c) It's not necessary to burn time and money on ALL the platforms if ONE platform is the best for your ideal customer After reading about the top five major social media platforms of today's world, start by picking ONE.

Pick one platform that your ideal customers love to predominantly use. Find them. Connect with them.

Meet me in the next chapter to find out WHAT to post for your ideal customers. We'll explore endless content ideas and start to build a content strategy.

THE BEST MARKETING DOESN'T FEEL LIKE MARKETING

— Tom Fishburne

Chapter Five: Making Your Content Stick!

Content marketing is a marketing strategy used to attract, engage, and retain an audience loyal to your brand through the art of copywriting, videos, photos, graphics, and other media formats.

Content marketing is simply a communication tool between you and your customers.

Content is a language. It's a message shared with your audience in a visual way.

Let's make your content stick!

Get it ;-)

I am going to share with you my Triple CCC formula:

Clear message + Creative content = Captive audience.

The clearer, more creative your message is, the more captive your audience will be.

The objective is to remember to implement the Triple C formula when creating your content ready for social media, and this is how:

Clear message

Is your message clear? Have you got a simple message that your audience is actually interested in?

Let's imagine, you are trying to attract first time buyers. You have decided you want to help first time buyers get on the property ladder, therefore your content needs to clearly speak to THIS audience.

What is an obviously clear message that this ideal customer will understand?

"We do mortgages for everyone"?

Or

"Helping first time buyers get out of the rent race and into their own home"?

Conversely, if you chose to target property developers and experienced landlords, which message would resonate most with them from the two options below?

"How to save a deposit in 6 simple steps"?

Or

"How to scale your property portfolio in a tax efficient way"?

You need to be clear on WHO you are trying to help and make the content relevant to them.

If your main customer base is made up of professional landlords, there is no point writing about 100% mortgages, saving a deposit, or explaining jargon. You have to assume that your sophisticated property investor already knows this and now has other pain points such as tax efficiency, diversification, best rates on the market, speedy lending decisions, and creative lending products.

Know your audience and make your content CLEAR. That is part one of the three Cs.

Let's look at part two.

Creative Content

Have you made it engaging? Using the art of copy combined with visuals such as video, photo, audio, and graphics, have you made your message captivating?

Now that you know WHAT you want to say, it's time to think about HOW you're going to say it.

This really is an art. There is a reason people have a full time copywriting job and that's because it takes mastery.

Copywriting and design are arts and take a lot of practice so I don't want to fool you into thinking that you will learn how to do this beautifully within this one chapter.

I would also argue at this point that it's not really in the mortgage adviser's realm to learn how to write and design. This is not an income producing activity like having a meeting with your clients and giving advice. This is definitely a task I would outsource to a professional, but more on this later.

For now, let me at least help you enough to get this off the ground. I will share a few quick top tips for making your content more engaging. A few simple methods to help you do it independently before needing to outsource.

→Short video content

In the previous chapter you learnt about the 5 major platforms. 4 out of those 5 are mainly about video content: Instagram Reels/Stories, Facebook Reels, YouTube Shorts, YouTube landscape videos, and TikToks. LinkedIn likes videos too but you can get away with just pictures and text on there at least to start with.

So, if 4 out of 5 major platforms prefer video, needless to say, video should be a must within your content strategy.

Make sure your videos range between 10 to 60 seconds that way they are suitable across all platforms. Whilst TikTok allows you to do up to 3 minutes, remember you can't post a 3-minute video on Instagram (at least that's where we are now at the time of writing this book) our videos should be recorded in portrait format because according to Zippia *"4.97 billion people worldwide access the internet with their mobile devices. This is about 90% of all global internet users."*

You don't need a super professional set up at first. You can certainly get away with the good old selfie angle, or a basic tripod with your smartphone.

Three absolute musts for your videos are: 1) Excellent lighting even if it's natural lighting. 2) Excellent audio quality 3) Punchy script. No waffling or long intros. Just get straight to the point and give the viewer a reason to continue watching.

Statistics have shown that you have on average 3 to 5 seconds to capture someone's attention to stop and watch your video. Once you have bought 5 seconds of their time, they will have decided whether to continue to watch your video.

Hootsuite has confirmed that on average people watch between 7 and 10 seconds.

Today, users like to consume MANY videos per day hence they prefer short snappy video clips. The shorter the clips, the more they consume.

We want to "binge watch" videos as fast as possible. Make your messages short and easy to absorb.

DON'T do this:

"Hi, it's Alex here … um … just wanted to jump on here real quick … um ... This is my first video so I hope you like it… um … I am the founder of Alex Mortgages and I am a fully qualified mortgage and protection adviser … Today I want to talk to you about …

I see the above opening video intros ALL THE TIME. It takes at least 10 seconds for this type of intro to finish, it's lacking substance and the speaker lacks confidence and comes across nervous.

If you have 3 to 5 seconds to captivate your audience, you need to tell them instantly why they should listen.

Instead, try the examples below.

Creative video opening hooks for you to try:

Why XXX is not working for you —> *Why your pension is not working for you …*

How to get X in 10 seconds → *How to think like the rich, in 10 seconds*

Let me show you the biggest life hack for… → *Let me show you the biggest life hack for saving a deposit for your first home*

Before you try XXX try this —> *Before you try to invest, try this...*

Instead of doing XXX try this instead → *Instead of investing in crypto, try this instead*

XXX life hack revealed —> *Homebuying life hack revealed ...*

The thing you've been missing in your XXXX —> *The thing you've been missing in your property portfolio strategy*

→ Images

Another way to make your content engaging other than videos, is pictures.

When I say pictures, I absolutely do not mean STOCK images.

I am going to vent now and then not mention it again because I think the point will be clear.

The reason I advise against stock footage of other people that are not you or your team members is because it looks like an ad. It looks generic, common, and overused.

Stock images of people are not engaging. You can instantly spot a fake person, team, or family a mile off. They look like models and therefore subconsciously tells your viewer "these are not real people".

You want to be recognisable and memorable. If you post fake people with your logo then who will be remembered?

If you are not seen then how can a customer associate your brand with you?

I suggest having the next following images in these 4 key categories that you should store in your content library:

1) You should have images that are candid. Natural pictures that you have taken with your phone. These could be of you in the office, with family, out enjoying yourself, taking part in a hobby, on holiday etc. Take pictures of everyday life.

Think back to Richard Branson.

We see Richard Branson like this:

And we see him like this:

If Richard Branson can build multiple multimillion-dollar businesses globally using his name, and showing his corporate and human side, so can you.

2) The second portfolio of images you need are professional. You need to hire a professional photographer to take headshots, media photos, PR photos and website photos.

When we do photoshoots for our clients, we make sure we capture: lifestyle, personal, professional, and media ready images.

If you are an adviser looking to get in the press either within or outside the industry, then you will need high resolution images ready for the media.

One of our wealth manager clients has been featured multiple times in different press publications including the Financial Times. He certainly couldn't get away with a 20-year-old photo back from his banking days, or a blurry selfie. We did a photoshoot to represent his sophisticated brand and positioned him as a thought leader.

Your website needs YOU not stock images. If you have a team, a cat, a dog, anybody within your business needs to be visible. You want to tell your business story with real people in the business.

As they say "pictures paint 1000 words".

Your images are crucial to the posts you create.

Seeing a picture of you regularly keeps your face and name front of mind.

I may not be ready to get a mortgage right now, or sort out my pension, but when I am ready your face will pop into my head. If I have seen it enough times to remember you.

I'll be thinking *"ah yes Sam could do my mortgage, I always see his posts and I am sure he can help".*

3) You also need images that are about your customers!!

Now this one is trickier… it's harder to get footage of your clients BUT have you asked? Chances are you haven't asked for a picture of them in their new home.

Why not try this: this month, next month, and the month after, ask ALL your new home owners who have moved into their home thanks to you, to take a little selfie at home. Ask them for their permission to be able to use it for social media purposes. I bet they will be happy to do so.

Think about it. They will be euphoric and delighted to have a new home thanks to you. They are at their happiest and will be more inclined to thank you with this small little favour.

Other than pictures of your clients, think about having pictures of their projects too!

If you work with landlords and property developers who renovate properties make sure you ask for permission to use their before, during, and after pictures. Turn these images into a case study and talk about how you helped them finance their renovation.

If you are actively working with a property developer on a big project, ask if you can visit the site?

My client, a commercial finance broker, took me to Nottingham to visit one of his clients who turned their farm into a luxury residential estate. We recorded video content on the day and took pictures to showcase the work. The client (the developer) and my client, the broker, were absolutely delighted. A great collaboration.

How can you do the same with your clients?

Make sure anything you do with clients is captured! Even if you go to a client's house warming party or a networking event, take regular pictures to capture you with real people!

4) Finally, you also need branded pictures.

You can create static text-based pictures through Canva. These images would have your branded colours, your logo, and a little bit of text as the header to clearly explain the purpose of the post i.e "100% mortgages are back: What you need to know" or "10 easy ways to save more money".

These images are not going to set social media on fire but they are helpful for your feed because it can give your page a very clear branded look. Just like your website, you need to decorate your social media page too. You can do this with real life pictures and with branded static posts.

The way I see these branded posts is they are there to give the audience a very quick menu summary of what you do and what you offer.

These images are also good to make announcements such as "United Kingdom Base Rate has risen"

cries

Let's now look at the final C.

Captive audience

Is your audience engaging? Are they interacting with your content? Most importantly, are you being social? Are YOU engaging with your audience beyond just posting on social media?

The final part of the triple C formula is building a Captive Audience.

We've been through Clear message, Creative content, now we will look at creating a Captive audience you engage with.

You don't need to be famous in order to build a phenomenal audience and business off the back of social media.

You just need to know a few people, who know a few people, who know a few people.

When you onboard a new client, you know that the lifetime value of that client and the referral opportunities off the back of that ONE client are invaluable.

It's not about doing 100 mortgages per month as a sole adviser. It's about doing one mortgage really well and then you'll get access to their family and friends which usually yield between 3 to 6 further clients off the back of 1 mortgage.

There's no point having 10k followers if you don't get them engaged.

Anybody can buy traffic, buy followers, or spam add everyone. But the value is in the engagement.

I don't consider myself to be famous by any stretch of the imagination. As it stands, I have 11k followers on LinkedIn, 700 on Instagram, 10k on one of my TikTok accounts and 200 on another TikTok account.

These numbers mean nothing if it wasn't for the fact that I actually get regular engagement and leads from social media.

The biggest satisfaction of all is walking into an industry event and suddenly everyone starts saying *"Is that the girl from LinkedIn?"* People actually feel like they KNOW me and then become a genuine connection not just another follower.

Whether I've had 100 or 10,000 followers, I have always treated everyone the same. I make sure I take time to engage with them, speak with them, even if just through social media or face to face at events.

I get so much pleasure from seeing my connections in real life. I make time to go to events and to meet and greet people within the financial services industry, so if you see me, please stop me to say hi and to have a cheeky selfie!

Do you engage with your audience on and off line?

Engagement isn't just about what happens on the phone, via email, or in a face to face meeting.

Look at social media like this: an online diary to document what you're doing and who you're with … that matters!

No, we don't need to see your food, or your kid's muddy football kit if it doesn't align with your brand and strategy.

Going to networking events, having face to face meetings with your clients etc, IS in line with your brand.

It's part of the show and tell, but not in a showy-off kind of way. It's about showcasing your knowledge, expertise, and connections because your clients care about the value you bring.

Showcasing that you have a busy schedule, and documenting your journey is valuable when you are telling a story about you and your brand.

It all links back to people getting to "know, like and trust you".

Content ideas to support this concept of "show and tell" and to further engage with your audience:

→ Going to a networking event? Take a few snaps of the meeting, a couple of selfies with some of the attendees, and then share your highlights and top tips on social media using those photos. Tag tag tag! Tag and thank the participants who attended the event. This opens up a line of communication online and creates more buzz post event.

→ 1 to 1 with a client in a coffee shop? Ask permission if you can take a cheeky selfie of the two of you and ask if you can thank them online for a lovely meeting. Keep it confidential. No need to post about their income and mortgage loan requirements. Simply say *"So excited to meet Sally today. Thanks for choosing us ABC Mortgage Ltd to do your mortgage. We can't wait for you to get your keys".*

→ Received a lovely gift from a client? Don't just take a picture of the chocolates… actually BE in the picture. Take a selfie with the gift because I am going to remember YOU not the chocolates. Take a picture of you with the gift and then tag your client and thank them openly on social media.

→ Lender visit? Has a business development manager come to visit you in the office to talk to you about their latest lender rates? Take a selfie of you and the lender. Tag them in the post. Show your client that you have access to decision makers AND you've got such a strong relationship with the lenders that they come to see you personally. This goes a long way. Client's love to see that you have access to small, large, famous, and niche lenders. This shows they can trust you because you have access to the right people.

Get the idea?

Try out the three options above.

There are two more ways to engage with your audience that I would like to share with you so stick with me a little longer.

We've discussed how you can post, tag people, include your clients, and other connections in your post.

Now we need to talk about engaging with other people's posts.

It's all well and good wanting to receive all the attention and the likes, but if you don't give it, why should you receive it?

If you want 100 likes, how many likes have you actually given?

It's the art of reciprocation. If you don't engage with others, then they aren't going to be thinking of engaging with you.

Make sure you make time to engage proactively with your ideal customer's posts.

If our client has appointed us to manage their social media profile and they tell us they want to generate more property developer clients, then we would typically engage with 20 to 30 new property developers per day on social media.

Who has time to do that, you say?

If I told you that there was a room filled with 100 first time buyers, would you want to be in that room?

If I told you that these first time buyers were going to be hanging out in my living room for the next couple of hours, wouldn't you want to try to talk to as many people in that room as possible?

Well you have been invited to a 24/7 FREE networking event taking place ONLINE where you have access to as many people as you like.

We typically would allocate 30 to 60 mins per day per client to ensure we were engaging with their ideal customer's content. This instigates organic traffic, likes, and followers.

You can do the same. If you are not ready to outsource this, then set aside just 20 to 30 minutes per day to engage with your potential clients.

What's the point of connecting with them if you don't talk to them?

Finally, the next best way to engage with your clients is to gamify the content.

For example, Instagram Stories give you the option to add gifs, polls, quizzes etc to the post. Help your followers engage with your content by giving them something fun and interactive.

<u>Quiz and Poll ideas:</u>

→ Post a picture of yourself and try out the Poll function through Instagram stories. Ask the audience *"Do you currently a) live at home with parents b) rent alone c) rent with partner d) own your own home"*

→ Post a picture of yourself in the Story and add the Quiz function through Instagram Stories. Ask the audience: *"What's the highest loan to value available for First Time Buyers? a) 90% b) 95% c) 100%"*

Your polls and quizzes don't just have to be about your products and services. You could ask for example:

"What content would you like to see more of?"
"What kind of merch would you appreciate?"
"What is your drink of choice on a sunny Friday afternoon?"
"How can we be more environmentally responsible in your opinion? Please send us suggestions."

You can also do polls on LinkedIn and Facebook.

By making your content more interactive, you're giving your audience more tools to play with and making your content more memorable because it makes the user have to think and interact rather than just scroll past.

That's the Triple C formula broken down. Now let's jump into further content ideas and how to ensure you never run out of them.

Chapter Six:
How To Think Of Content Ideas

Have you found yourself at this point in the book thinking *"This has been great up until now, I am learning how to build my brand and how to use the social media platforms, BUT... what on earth do I post?"*

I have peppered a lot of content ideas throughout this book already. I have suggested styles, titles, and ideas which I hope you have picked up on so far.

In this chapter I am going to share with you my 7 Content Pillars for a buzzing content marketing strategy.

In order to bring your strategy to life, you need content ideas!

Struggling to think of what to post?

Follow my 7-step guide to never running out of ideas again!

I will break this down into my 7 Pillars of Content Ideas.

Whenever you can't think of what to post, refer back to these pillars. These will prompt you to think of an idea based on each category.

Pillar 1: Start with You

I'll keep saying it, people buy from people.

Your unique stories and experiences cannot be copied. You hold the copyright to your own stories and only you can begin to tell them.

Whilst there is plenty of content out there that can be modified to suit your own business, your story is your story.

This is what makes your brand unique.

Your story is your Unique Selling Point.

I've lost you…

I can already hear you saying:

"I don't want to talk about me, I want to talk about the business"

"I don't want to share my personal story, I want to grow the business brand"

"I want to keep personal and business separate"

I am not talking about sharing your deepest darkest secrets or exposing your fears.

I am not suggesting you open up old wounds or air out your dirty laundry.

When I was working for a specialist lender, this is how I viewed my personal brand versus the company I was working for:

→ The company name was the product. Who I worked for was the "hat" I was wearing at the time, so to speak.

→ The personal brand, therefore me, was the one nurturing the relationship. The personal brand was the one driving the traction and attention towards the product, whilst building the relationship.

Prior to working for a specialist lender, I worked for a packager, as I mentioned in the intro.

When I moved from the packager to the lender, what changed? The company name, therefore the product, changed. I stayed the same.

I visited many brokers during my years as a Business Development Manager (BDM), and the one thing that stayed the same no matter where I was working, was me.

I was the fixed product they bought into. I was the person they built trust with NOT the name of the company I worked for.

Where you work changes.

WHO you are doesn't.

Can you relate? Let me ask you this…

When you were a mortgage adviser, or a financial adviser, working for somebody else and then decided to go solo, did you want your customers to follow you?

When you used to work for a large, corporate financial firm (if you did) where leads were provided to you and you were just a number out of hundreds of advisers, did you decide to leave because you wanted to be YOURSELF?

Did you leave a larger firm to become your own boss?

Do you have customers who follow you regardless of where you work?

Whether you want to build a personal brand or not, you already have one. You already have a brand.

People follow people, not companies.

CONTENT is what you use on social media to convey that message and bring your brand to the forefront.

For example: When I was working with the lender, the product criteria were VERY complex, especially because advisers weren't used to using this particular lender. It was not a mainstream lender, not to mention quite expensive, so advisers were apprehensive about using their product.

Enter... business development managers. It's the business development managers who brings the product to life! Without them, it would be very difficult for the company to grow organically. The company requires a human to explain the features and benefits to the adviser, AND to bond with the adviser to build trust. This is what then makes the product more understandable.

The same goes for financial advisers. The world of money, investments, savings, pensions, mortgages, equity release, and protection is complex. It can be overwhelming. There are many COMPANIES to choose from but only one of YOU. Use the power of your personal brand to connect with your audience.

So how do you build content around Pillar 1?

Pick three to five pivotal moments in your life that have shaped you into the business owner that you are.

I am suggesting to pick up to five features about YOURSELF that make you a real human who people see themselves working with and FOR.

If you had a room full of customers (or friends and family if you do not have any clients yet), what would they say about you if you weren't in the room?

If you are a team of one and eventually see yourself hiring more brokers whether self-employed or employed, this will help you to also build your EMPLOYER brand. If you aspire to grow into a larger brokerage and not a single adviser firm, advisers will want to know WHO they are working for. They will want to get to know you as a business owner of the brokerage before deciding whether or not to join you.

Did you know that, according to HubSpot research, the average time somebody spends on a website is 62 seconds? And did you also know that the four most visited pages on a website, still according to HubSpot, are: Home page, About page as the 2nd most important, followed by Blog and then Contact Us.

This shows that the majority of website traffic is about learning as much as possible about the company AND THE PEOPLE, before getting in touch.

Make every second count.

We suggest this to ALL our clients *"Make sure you have a standout About Me and Team profile on your website, which can also be repeated on social media pages".*

The second thing I suggest you do therefore is to rewrite your personal bio to use for the website, social media, and the press.

So how can you do this whilst keeping a fine balance between being personable and professional?

Task: What personal stories throughout your life are pivotal to your career?

Don't go right back to when you were 5 and lost your tooth but you are traumatised by the lack of money the tooth fairy didn't bring to you.

Think about the life changing events in your life which have pushed you to become who you are.

Approach this from a place of strength. Feel empowered by your story. Feel empowered by your WHY.

Here are the key questions to guide you:

Why do you do what you do?

Did you become a parent? How does this feel?

Did you start your own business because *enter your frustration here*

Did you start your own business because *enter your aspirations here*

Have you achieved a milestone you're incredibly proud of? Why? What relevance does this have to your audience and why should they care?

Do you have a particular skill or expertise that sets you apart from the rest?

What are your interests and hobbies? Do you partake in world changing aspirational events such as saving the planet? Do you volunteer in schools? Do you manage a football team on a Saturday?

The answers to the questions above, will help you to understand more about yourself. These are talking points with your customers.

For example: If your story is *"I left a big corporate advisory firm because I didn't feel heard or valued, so I decided to start up my own advice firm where every single client would feel empowered and loved under my caring service."*

Now you can share content around:

- Company values
- Why customers come first
- Happy customer reviews and testimonials
- What it was like to start your own business. How did you find the courage to do it?
- What motivates you?
- What are the challenges you encountered when starting a business?

Create content to match the answers you have given in the questions above.

At this point I will mention that you do not need 365 new content ideas per year. You don't need to keep saying something NEW every day. In fact, quite the opposite.

These answers you have formulated form part of the core values and therefore messaging of your business.

You want to stick to the core messaging as much as possible and keep reminding your audience about it.

Don't just mention the message ONCE and expect your audience to remember. Keep reminding your audience of the same core messages by changing the way in which you write about it and the imagery you use to go with your message.

Change the asset NOT the core message.

(By asset I mean: the video, the article, the blog, the piece of content that you've designed to share the message)

As we say in Manuka Media, "Content that sticks". Make it memorable, sweet, and sticky... like Honey!

Pillar 2: Listen to Your Customers

Your customers are the best content creators!

If your content doesn't speak your customer's language, it's lost on them. Your content won't attract their attention if you are not directing the message to them.

Do you ever feel like your phone is listening to you?

I am sure you have been in that spooky situation before where you've just been speaking to your colleague or friend about this amazing new *insert here any object* and then you pick up your phone and suddenly there's an ad for it?

Have you then noticed that you keep seeing that THING everywhere? Your neighbour has it, you see it on Facebook, Instagram, and then you even get emails about it!

You finally cave and buy it because it's constantly at the forefront of your mind.

That's how it should feel with your customers.

1. They should feel like they see you everywhere.
2. Secondly, they should feel like YOU have the answer to their problem.
3. They should feel like you have exactly what they are looking for.

Let's make this example relevant to mortgages or pensions.

Your customer, Alex, is a professional landlord. They have several properties and are looking to make the portfolio more profitable. With the new tax laws, inflation, and interest rates rising, they are finding themselves losing money.

You start posting on social media. You make blogs for your website. You send out newsletters. You tick all the marketing boxes because you know that's what you're supposed to do to get new customers.

But ... you talk a lot about "How to save a deposit", "How to get on the property ladder", "How to buy your first BTL", "100% mortgages are back".

Is this for your ideal customer Alex?

Does Alex pay attention to this content you are posting?

Do they find it relevant and feel compelled to engage?

No, would be the correct answer.

Alex is looking for specific information to solve their problem that is relevant to an experienced landlord and not a first-time buyer.

If you did want to attract first time buyers instead of more people like Alex, then continue posting away as per the example above. However, if you want to keep your customers who are like Alex, then you need to be producing content that they would appreciate.

Alex would appreciate more content like this for example:

1. *How to make your rental properties increase in value with these 3 easy steps*
2. *How to improve the rental yield of your property with this super hack*
3. *This is the trick you've been missing to maximise the value of your portfolio*
4. *Why your properties are dropping in value, and what you need to do about it*
5. *3 ways to make sure you are being tax efficient in property*

These subject matters and problem areas would certainly make Alex pay attention, don't you agree?

Now your turn.

If you want to produce content your customers would appreciate then get to know your customer.

In chapter 1, I helped you through the ideal customer avatar exercise. From that exercise, you should now be much clearer about your customers' pains, challenges, desires, and motivations.

Using the pains and motivations your customers have, brainstorm content that you think would help answer those burning questions they have.

Exercise: Go through these 2 questions below as prompts to get you thinking about content suitable for your ideal customer and look at the right column for further hints.

1) What questions do you constantly get on repeat from customers?

Listen out for:

"What documents do I need for.."

"How much can I borrow if…"

*"What does *insert jargon here* mean?"*

2) When you get an enquiry either via email, text, socials, or telephone, what does the client SAY to you? What do they tell you they are struggling with?

Listen out for:

"I was recommended to come to you because you helped XYZ with …"

"I have been really stuck on …"

"I am currently unable to …"

"I really want to … but…."

Pillar 3: Using AI and Other Software

I am sure you want to know: *"What content is actually popular and likely to get traction?"*

I can hear you saying: *"Tell me what works. Tell me exactly what I should post"*.

There's been a lot of attention poured into ChatGPT and Bard by the general public looking to see if these platforms could massively improve their lives through automation.

For example, many have attempted to use ChapGPT as a source of content material for example.

I am not averse to the idea of utilising these powerful tools to help with marketing strategies.

In fact, if you actually DON'T know what to say, how to write, or you are uninspired, then perhaps ChatGPT could start to loosen up your creative thinking.

The way I see ChatGPT is that it is an instigator. It's a starting point.

If you have picked an ideal customer to be a first time buyer for example, you could use ChatGPT to ask it: *"Hey ChatGPT, what do first time buyers want to know about the homebuying process?"*

For example, I typed this exact question into the website and this is what came back:

First-time home buyers often have a range of questions and concerns when it comes to the homebuying process. Here are some common topics they typically want to know about:

1. *Affordability: First-time buyers often want to understand how much they can afford and what factors affect their affordability, such as down payments, mortgage rates, and monthly mortgage payments. They may seek information on calculating their budget and understanding loan options.*
2. *Financing and Mortgages: Buyers are often curious about the various types of mortgages available to them, including fixed-rate and adjustable-rate mortgages. They may want to know about pre-approval processes, interest rates, loan terms, and the necessary documentation for obtaining a mortgage.*
3. *Home Search: First-time buyers may have questions about how to start their home search, including factors to consider when choosing a location, working with real estate agents, browsing listings, attending open houses, and making informed decisions about their preferences and needs.*
4. *Offer and Negotiation: Buyers typically want to know how to make an offer on a property and navigate the negotiation process. They may have questions about determining an appropriate offer price, contingencies, inspection and appraisal processes, and strategies for successful negotiations.*

5. *Closing Process: Understanding the steps involved in the closing process is crucial. First-time buyers often seek information about home inspections, title searches, escrow accounts, and the roles of various parties involved, such as real estate agents, attorneys, lenders, and closing agents.*
6. *Additional Costs: Buyers should be aware of the additional costs associated with purchasing a home, such as closing costs, property taxes, homeowners insurance, and potential ongoing expenses like maintenance, repairs, and utilities.*
7. *Government Programs and Assistance: First-time buyers may want to learn about any government programs or assistance available to help them with down payments, closing costs, or other aspects of the homebuying process. They could inquire about FHA loans, VA loans, or other local or state programs.*
8. *Home Inspections and Appraisals: Understanding the importance of home inspections and appraisals is crucial. Buyers may want to know what these processes entail, how to find reputable professionals, and how the results can impact their decision-making.*
9. *Legal and Contractual Obligations: First-time buyers should familiarise themselves with the legal and contractual aspects of purchasing a home, such as reviewing and understanding the purchase agreement, contingencies, and disclosures.*
10. *Homeownership Responsibilities: Buyers often seek information about the responsibilities of homeownership, such as property maintenance, homeowners association (HOA) fees, and understanding the rules and regulations of the community they are buying into.*

Remember, each buyer's situation may vary, and it's important for them to consult with professionals such as real estate agents, mortgage lenders, and attorneys to get personalised advice and guidance throughout the homebuying process.

I'll let you be the judge of this copy and how effective you think it would be for your customers. I left the answer ChaptGPT gave me unedited. I haven't amended anything because I wanted to show you the quality of the answer to the question I asked.

That's my warning to you.

The answer is only as good as the question it is given. Be specific and always proofread.

Secondly, ChatGPT can only give you standard generic answers which will not carry your tone and style. Use this platform as a way to generate ideas with a view to applying your own knowledge and personality to the content.

Trending content

Diving deeper into this section, pillar 3, let's explore other ways you could be creating content with AI and automation tools.

There is a free online tool which auto suggests content ideas for you that have been sourced and generated using site data from Google and Bing. These content suggestions are popular searches made by the general public on search engines such as Google and Bing.

Huh?

Let me explain more if this is your first time.

You go to a site called Answerthepublic.com.

Type in a key word or phrase you think your ideal customer might be searching for such as "mortgages for self-employed".

The tool then generates the most searched for phrases with those keywords.

The tool then generates hundreds to thousands of frequently asked questions that your ideal customers have been searching for on Google and Bing.

These searches should form part of your core content marketing strategy. You should be listening to your actual customers (pillar 2) as well as what the search engines are picking up on.

After all, 88% of people go to Google first when they have a problem.

This pillar alone, as well as number 2, will keep you busy for at least 1 year with endless creative content ideas.

But the key is … implementation.

You'll feel like you've struck gold with this platform because "the thinking" is done for you. You have content ideas staring right at you but the hard work is putting them into action.

Just because you've found the top 25 trending questions on Google within your keyword research, doesn't mean you will start to appear on page one of Google overnight.

Like anything, consistency, volume, and quality are essential.

The reason copywriting feels like a big job is because it is. It takes a lot of experience, creativity, and volume to make the content stick.

Posting 25 articles on your website and hoping they will reach your audience far and wide just won't cut it.

Posting 25 pictures on social media with the relevant hashtags won't bring in two enquiries per day.

These content ideas are just that, ideas.

You need to use these ideas as part of your wider marketing and communication strategy.

Think about these ideas when you are:

- Creating newsletters
- Recording videos

- Producing an Ebook
- Posting social media content

Whenever you are creating any visual or written material, you must consider these results from Answerthepublic.com if you want to speak your customer's language and give them exactly what they want.

With this platform, you know for sure that your message is hitting the mark.

Now, it's down to:

1) how well you write it
2) how you make it visually engaging and
3) how much content you are able to produce on a consistent basis to ensure it makes an impact.

Pillar 4: Keep an Eye Out for the Competition

You are not alone.

Your colleagues, other mortgage brokers or financial advisers, will be actively trying to promote themselves too on social media.

By no means am I suggesting you copy them.

Absolutely not.

Neither am I saying you need to be like them.

In fact, I would suggest having a clear out of your socials and remove as many competitors from your connection list as possible. There's no point being connected to a bunch of other mortgage brokers who are not your clients!

Pillar 4 is simply an inspiration tool just in case you get stuck on creating your next content idea.

Having a sneak peek at what the competition is doing wouldn't hurt.

We all do it...

In fact, it does truly inspire me. I get excited seeing my competitors do well because it gives me a rocket to get moving! It stops me being complacent. It fuels my passion even more.

COMPARISON IS THE THIEF OF JOY

—Theodore Roosevelt

Notice how I haven't said "compare yourself to your competitors".

I am simply suggesting you pick 2 or 3 icons in your industry that you look up to as a way to guide you and remind you of what you should be doing.

It's healthy to have a little competition.

Following a couple of your industry icons helps you sharpen the saw, as said by Steven Covey in his book, 7 Habits of Highly Effective people.

Look to them to see their style, their form of delivery, their messaging etc. Learn from the best and then apply this knowledge to your own position.

You will always be different from them because you are YOU.

Pillar 5: Think Outside the Box

Another place to get content ideas is OUTSIDE of the industry.

We all know Financial Services has been a bit late in adopting social media so needless to say, creativity is still developing in this space.

This means that you need to use the power of "outside the box thinking".

Find another industry outside of financial services that you love. Fitness? Food? Fashion? Beauty? Sport?

Check out leading influencers, brands, and general content from those other industries that you love and see how they do it.

How do these other leading brands in the sector you've chosen, market themselves?

How do these influencers use the power of storytelling to move people to buy a certain product?

If you want to get really creative, try to use analogies inspired by other industries and apply it to financial services.

How can you use something relatable and mainstream, and bring it to the world of mortgages, pensions, equity release, protection, and investments?

Pillar 6: Current Affairs & Industry News

It's impossible to run out of things to post about when there is always something going on in the news.

One very easy way to find content ideas is to keep a lookout in the media.

I am not one to watch the news on TV because it can be quite depressing, but we certainly can keep up to date with current affairs in many different ways.

Think, local / national / and global.

Let's think local first.

What is happening in your area?

I am going to use my client here as an example (anonymous of course).

Client, a wealth manager from Norfolk. Whilst on a national level he's been featured in the Financial Times, he has also been spotted in the local press too.

As we manage his social media accounts, we have been targeting local groups in Norfolk to build up relationships in the local community.

This wealth manager has an office in Norfolk and lives there too, so it made sense to get to know local publications, groups, communities, networking events, and also local businesses.

By being aware of the local events, he has been able to sponsor an Under 11s football team for example, and he's also been able to attend local events to give talks. He's set up introducer relationships with local accountants too!

What more could you be doing in your local area?

Perhaps there are networking or sponsorship opportunities you could take advantage of and then talk about it on social media!

The magic of collaboration projects like this is that YOU post about it, and THEY post about it too. This means it increases the traction on your profile and visibility.

Whenever you are stuck, think of ways you could reach out into the current affairs of the world whether on a local or national level, and find ways to make it relevant to your business so you can post about it.

Don't just post about "National chocolate day" because it's national chocolate day.

Actually find meaningful events in the world that make a difference to your audience and your business.

Last but not least, industry news.

We have endless publications and news reports flying around the financial world.

Don't assume your customers know what is going on.

If you haven't posted this week and are struggling to think of ideas, read the latest newsletters your lenders have sent you.

Have a look at the industry publications such as Mortgage Strategy, Financial Reporter, Mortgage Introducers, Bridging & Commercial, etc, and pick out interesting stories, facts, and news that you think could be relevant to your audience.

As financial advisers, you get hot off the press news with all things property, lending, protection, and other interesting stories from various providers.

Again! Don't assume your customers know what is happening in your world.

Share with them what you know!

Please do not simply repost an article released by the BBC Money section.

Do not reshare the article by Mortgage Strategy.

You need to be sharing your OWN commentary.

Take inspiration, notes, and facts from the content you are reading, and then turn it into your own!

You should absolutely cite the original content creator but put your own spin on it. Show your influence by having your own opinion.

Pillar 7: Trust Tags

Pillar 7 is my next favourite pillar after Pillar 1. This is because Pillar 7 adds gravitas. It counterbalances more of the "softer" more personable posts, with the punchier *"I said I was good and here's the proof"* kinda posts.

Trust tags basically means: being associated with other reputable people and brands.

This pillar will inspire you to post about the winning accolades, milestones, big and small wins your customers need to see.

Pillar 7 is about building authority, conveying your influence, and building trust.

Done incorrectly, and you just come across like a show off. Nobody wants that…

Most finance professionals ONLY post when they win an award, or receive a fancy gift from a client, or talk about their latest press release. You only ever see the HIGHS on their feed and none of the other stuff such as: the journey, the value-added educational posts, the fun posts, the lows, etc.

Some finance professionals wrongly assume that because they are "serious" people or "senior" "professional people" that they should only show this side of themselves. That's why they disappear off the social media radar until they want to "brag" for want of a better word.

I can see the rationale. Don't get me wrong. I totally appreciate that people would only want to show the good stuff on social media but … this does not actually make you credible or relatable.

As the saying goes "nobody likes a show off" so use this pillar with caution.

This pillar is supposed to back up all the other posts (pillars 1 to 6) with the seal of approval. It's there to evidence and demonstrate the weight your story holds.

You absolutely should scream and shout from the rooftops if you win an award and even if you are simply nominated and shortlisted! It's something to be super proud of. Definitely share it.

When you get featured in the press, share it!

When you get invited to be a guest speaker, share it!

Share it all!

Perhaps you might be thinking at this stage, "only the big firms win these awards", "People pay for these awards and trophies" "I'll never get one of these".

You are mistaken.

I have seen big event sponsors walk home with zero. Nada. Zilch.

Equally, I have seen never-heard-of-before brokers walk away with a trophy at "best broker" when nobody had heard of them.

I am proof of this too!!

Back in 2019, when I was flying high as a business development manager and building my career with no projections of a business on the horizon, I was nominated in the Financial Reporter Women's Recognition Awards (WRA19). I came top 3 in the Rising Star category. I'd only been a BDM for that lender for 1 year and I was already making my mark. BUT I certainly didn't pay for it. I couldn't…

I was shortlisted on merit. I applied because the marketing team at Financial Reporter told me to! They spotted me at an event and suggested I should go for it.

I applied with a manifesto and then had to also submit some testimonials. The winner was chosen by a panel of judges.

No, I didn't win, but the nomination will stay with me for a lifetime.

Of course I have shared this multiple times on my socials and at speaking events. It makes me proud and shows just how valued I am by the people around me who believed enough in me.

That's the feeling I wish for you.

If you are not pushing yourself to go for these awards, then please do.

Please put yourself forward and let go of expectations. Watch just how magical this could be.

You win some, you lose some.

YOU MISS
100%
OF THE
SHOTS
YOU DON'T
TAKE

~ Wayne Gretzky ~

When you have been featured in Mortgage Introducer, Mortgage Strategy, and Financial Reporter to mention a few, that is showing your audience you have influence in the industry.

When you've been featured in the Financial Times, or even your local newspaper, that shows your audience you know what you're talking about.

When you are seen at elite networking events, that shows your audience that you network with the right people in the right places.

You want your audience to like you as a person, and respect you as a business professional.

That is perfect harmony.

To be known, liked, and trusted as an all rounded person. You're not just a braggy award winner, but a nice person too.

It's hard to find nice people...

Playing small never helped anybody.

There are many who choose to be quietly successful. That's okay. You can still grow a phenomenal business without having to tell your wider network or community.

The win is not important.

I am not going to say that "it's the taking part that counts" to you. I know you don't need me to sugarcoat the failures or near misses.

The reason I am so passionate about trust tags is because it elevates your influence.

One career highlight of mine when it comes to trust tags is working with Female Invest. They approached me out of the blue via LinkedIn and I nearly dismissed the opportunity for wrongly thinking it was spam.

Female Invest, for those who have not come across them, is a financial education and community platform, dedicated to empowering women to achieve financial success and closing the financial gender gap.

They sent this:

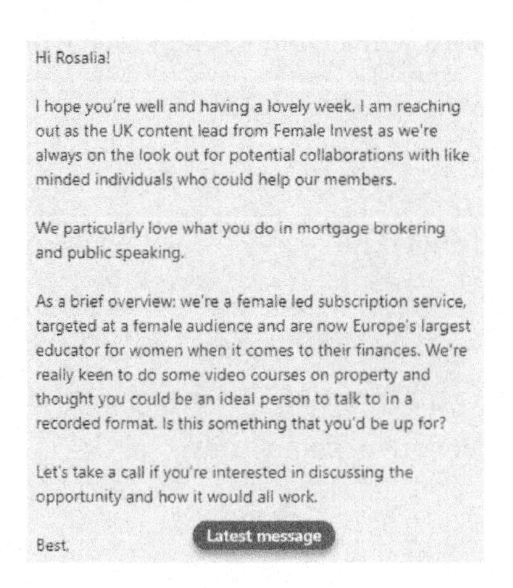

Hi Rosalia!

I hope you're well and having a lovely week. I am reaching out as the UK content lead from Female Invest as we're always on the look out for potential collaborations with like minded individuals who could help our members.

We particularly love what you do in mortgage brokering and public speaking.

As a brief overview: we're a female led subscription service, targeted at a female audience and are now Europe's largest educator for women when it comes to their finances. We're really keen to do some video courses on property and thought you could be an ideal person to talk to in a recorded format. Is this something that you'd be up for?

Let's take a call if you're interested in discussing the opportunity and how it would all work.

Best,

Latest message

I thought it was SPAM!!

I genuinely thought *"that's not ME who they want to work with. They are just scouting for volunteers. This must be a template message they send to everyone"*.

But I was wrong.

Turns out they knew me so well that they had also listened to the The Money Honey podcast and as I have been a speaker and an advocate for women in finance and financial education in general, they wanted to collaborate with my brand!!

This was their follow up message to the very excited (and high pitched) voice note I sent to them:

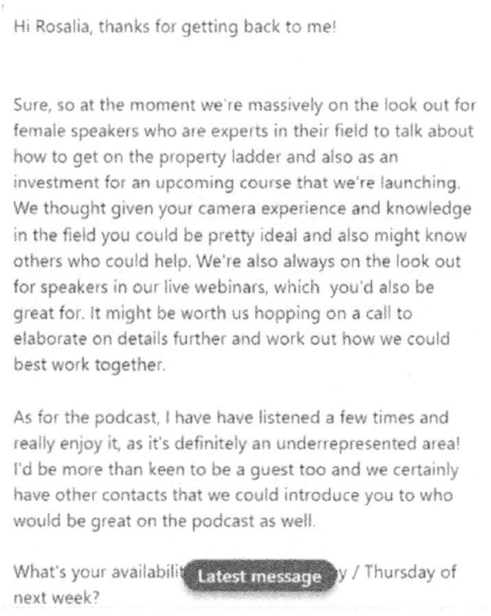

Hi Rosalia, thanks for getting back to me!

Sure, so at the moment we're massively on the look out for female speakers who are experts in their field to talk about how to get on the property ladder and also as an investment for an upcoming course that we're launching. We thought given your camera experience and knowledge in the field you could be pretty ideal and also might know others who could help. We're also always on the look out for speakers in our live webinars, which you'd also be great for. It might be worth us hopping on a call to elaborate on details further and work out how we could best work together.

As for the podcast, I have have listened a few times and really enjoy it, as it's definitely an underrepresented area! I'd be more than keen to be a guest too and we certainly have other contacts that we could introduce you to who would be great on the podcast as well.

What's your availabili Latest message y / Thursday of next week?

CONTENT BUILDS RELATIONSHIPS.
RELATIONSHIPS ARE BUILT ON TRUST.
TRUST DRIVES REVENUE.
— Andrew Davis

Chapter Seven: The 7 Deadly Sins Of What Not To Do On Social Media

In this age of incessant connectivity, where attention spans are dwindling and information overload reigns supreme, it is crucial to understand the potential pitfalls you may encounter when entering the dark layers of social media.

Welcome to Chapter 7 as we unveil the shadows that lurk beneath its vibrant surface. In this chapter, we delve into the seven deadly sins of what not to do on social media.

From explosive comment wars to ill-advised rants, we expose the dangers that lie in letting wrath consume your digital presence.

Greed takes centre stage as we unravel the consequences of shameless self-promotion and the pursuit of empty validation. The dangers of sloth follow, as inaction breeds missed opportunities and personal stagnation.

This chapter will help you confront the sins of gluttony, lust, and pride, witnessing the pitfalls of excessive consumption, objectification, and the relentless chase for admiration.

How do you maintain a level head, a clean reputation, and a thriving business without letting the greed, pride, and gluttony suck you into the digital realm?

1. Worshipping Vanity Metrics

I have a bee in my bonnet about this so let's just address it once and for all.

The definition of Vanity Metrics is: *statistics that look fantastic on the surface but don't necessarily translate into any meaningful business results.*

Vanity Metrics such as a high follower count and likes make you look good, but might have very little substance.

You. Do. Not. Need. Millions. Of. Followers. To. Be. "Successful". On. Social. Media.

Make sure you get specific about what you will measure on social media and how you will recognise success.

From day one, set out your metrics and decide what you intend to gauge.

If you are only focused on the number of likes and followers then you have missed the point. You will end up disappointed for a while and miss all the little wins and milestones.

How many followers is enough?

1,000?
10,000?
1m?
10m?

How many followers would you need to consider yourself "successful?"

How many likes do you need before you can be satisfied that social media works?

This is a dangerous zone. If you only ever recognise the likes and followers, you will miss all the other amazing opportunities.

Remember to count all the small wins too! Remember to value ALL your followers.

How you treat 10 followers should be how you treat 10,000 followers!

Don't forget the people who started with you. Don't forget the people who have been with you since day one. Without them, the compound effect wouldn't kick in.

10, will turn into 100, 100 will be 1000 and so on. Nurture these followers from day 1 and appreciate them.

Even during my early days of starting the business, when I had 2,000 RANDOM followers and on average 50 likes, I reached a healthy six figure business within 14 months.

I say 'random' because I wasn't using my LinkedIn for business as I was always employed so I had a mixture of connections. Now that I am a business owner, I have a different motive for LinkedIn.

Now that I have 11,000+ followers at the time of writing this, I still don't feel "famous" but my goodness the magic has been insane.

The connections, collaborations, clients, and friends I have cultivated in just three short years since starting my business (2020 - 2023) have been mind blowing. I have achieved more than I ever thought was possible even with a few hundred followers when I first started.

My level of following in comparison to MollyMae 7.5 million, Steven Barlett 2.5 million, Gary Vee 10 million, and Oprah 22.5 million to mention a few, is not even noticeable.

Vanity Metrics steal your ability to value your self worth.

Stay in your lane and measure the value, not the volume.

Don't get me wrong. I don't want you to walk away from this thinking that I do not keep an eye out for the growth of my accounts or the reach my posts are getting.

I don't want you to think that I am dismissing the numbers on my client's account.

The two points I am trying to make are:

1. What do the numbers mean? Are they converting into value?
2. You don't need to be famous to be generating business on social media. You can make the numbers count even if you are starting with 200, 500, or 5,000+ followers.

Of course I love it when I get new followers BUT only if they are the RIGHT audience.

I would rather get one new mortgage broker following me, than 1000 new random users with obscure names, who have a dummy account.

I would rather get 50 likes from leading financial institutions in my network, than 145k views on my TikTok from people all over the world I do not know.

The numbers only matter if you can do something with it. Focus on the client demographic rather than the number.

Pay attention to the names of people who like your LinkedIn and Instagram posts and sense check that they are your ideal customer.

When you get 50 likes, and 40 of them are from your ideal customer and NOT your competitor, that's how you know the content is working.

I love numbers. I love the analytics tools on social media platforms. These tools tell where my audience traffic is coming from, who is engaging with my post etc. It enables me to keep an eye on who is landing on my page and interacting. It confirms that the message is landing in the right place.

> Try this: set some goal outside of numbers. What do you want to achieve on social media? Who do you want to network with? What are your weakest skills that you would like to improve on, i.e Reels? Set yourself personal targets too such as developing your speaker confidence and video skills. These are great milestones too.

2. Spamming

The second deadly sin is spamming.

Spam adding.
Spam messaging.
Spam commenting.

Be careful not to get trigger happy when adding new followers and connections. Be mindful who you are connecting with and actually spend time engaging with them before adding hundreds of people to your profile with no real meaningful interaction.

I like to say hello to all my new connections as quickly as possible. If someone has added me or followed me, it means they must be interested in getting to know me and the business BUT this is not an invitation to send them a sales pitch.

That's spam.

If every time you connect with someone you send them a pre-scripted sales message then that's going to put your new connection off.

At this point, I shall mention that I actually don't mind automation. Bear with me…

Automation tools used in the right way are really not wrong.

Sending out a mail shot, scheduling a post, setting your out of office on, that's automation! It's no different to connecting with your audience and sending them an automated message saying "hello."

What's worse in your opinion: manually typing out a scripted sales pitch and sending it to your new follower? Or, automating a message saying "thanks for connecting, how are you?"

Notice the difference?

People have been shaming automation because they think that's spam BUT done properly in a human way, it actually doesn't feel like spam at all.

It's not actually the automation that's wrong, it's what you say.

Whether you do it manually or you automate it, make sure you make it meaningful and not salesy.

Here is an example of spammy message which is SALESY, from an actual financial adviser no other:

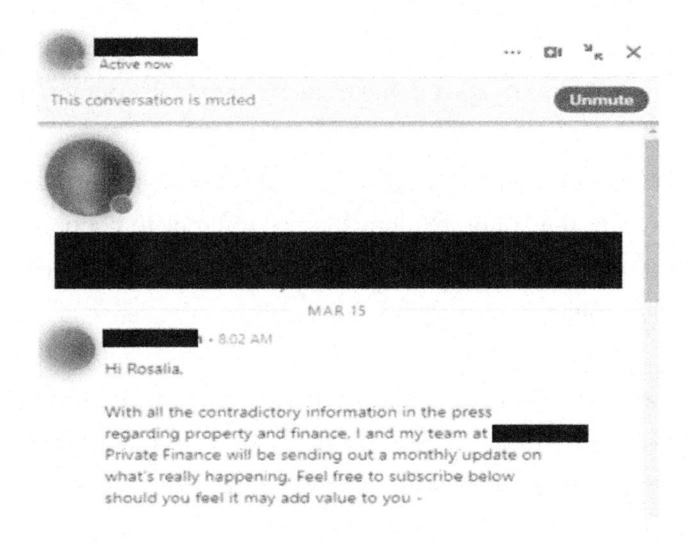

As you can see from the picture. I have muted this chat because they are constantly sending chunky scripted paragraphs to me trying to sell me financial advice. Their admin or automation person clearly sends the same message to ALL of his contacts without prequalifying the audience.

One thing is sending the same message to ALL potential clients, another is sending the same message to all RANDOM people.

Do this instead. Here is an example of me sending a non-salesy message to my ideal customer avatar, and getting a lead!

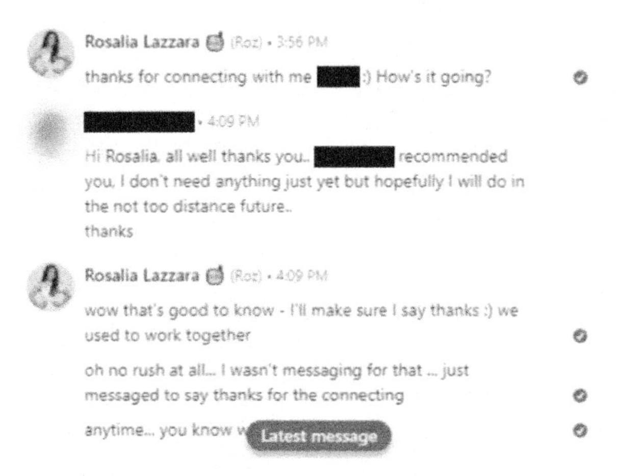

This is how the lead came about:

1. Person connected with me
2. I made the first move and sent them a thank you message
3. They replied and told me that they heard about me from someone else and they would eventually get in touch with me

4. I thanked her and then LEFT HER ALONE. I didn't send a proposal, pitch deck, rate card etc.
5. Now that I know they are interested, I keep them on my radar. I engage with their content.

3 months later …

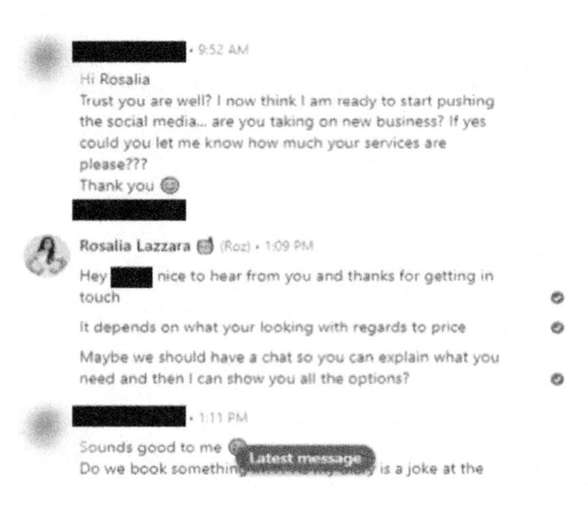

Once they were ready to buy, they got in touch with me. And that's how it's done…

Your new connections won't always be ready to buy straight away. Especially things as big as a mortgage or a new retirement plan!

They need to build up trust and knowledge around you first. They also need to consider certain options and eventually be at the right stage when they can actually buy from you. Let them go through that journey but make sure you nurture them through it.

Don't just add people for the sake of adding them. Make sure you research your target audience and build your network with the right people.

Try this:

Make a list of all your recent enquiries. How many do you have? 12? 20? 200? Work through that list on a daily basis. Spend 5 to 10 minutes looking up their names on social media. Are they on Facebook? LinkedIn? Instagram? Do they have a business page you could like and follow? Add these people on social platforms and engage with their content. Send them a message when they have connected with you. Maybe saying *"thanks for calling us at ABC mortgages. It was a pleasure to speak with you and good luck with your house search."*

3. Not engaging

As I alluded to in the previous sin, not engaging is criminal.

Engagement is split in two parts. One, you being proactive and engaging with other accounts. Two, making your content engaging.

I want to remind you again that engagement is paramount. The more engagement your posts get, the more the algorithm recognises that your content is valuable and therefore shares it to a wider audience.

The social media platforms want to keep their audience engaged and hooked on social media so your posts need to tick this box.

Equally you also need to be active on the platform and engage with others.

The algorithm only works if you work it. Engagement is the key to unlocking your account's algorithm potential.

Engagement takes many forms such as:

- Tagging people and being tagged in a post
- Gamification of posts such as polls, quizzes, giveaways etc
- Private chat with connections
- Commenting on people's posts and starting a conversation
- Adding people to your network
- Reactions to posts such as likes, love hearts etc.

Let's look at examples of how you can make your content more engaging with the use of polls, quizzes, and attention-grabbing giveaways.

Give away competition: I am going to use one of my early customers as an example for this one. They are mortgage brokers in Essex.

Their ideal customers are parents, typically between 36 and 44 years old. They have a very large network of friends and teachers. They have children themselves so they often network with other parents and meet new people all the time through friends of friends.

Their best performing platform is Facebook! They tend to stay in touch with their friends and other parents through Facebook and Facebook groups.

Their other best performing lead generation method is to engage in all the school events and functions, host parties for children, and attend other children's birthdays.

I ran a Facebook campaign for them which was a huge hit! The purpose of it was to engage their existing audience whilst expanding their reach to new potential customers and tapping into their friends' network.

Given that their ideal audience is parents and children, we ran a campaign around "Back to school" with a free Tablet giveaway during lockdown back in January 2021.

This is what we wrote in the launch post:

"Home schooling? Working from home? Trying to juggle work and life during lockdown?

Let us help you by giving your children the tools they need to make home learning a little more comfortable

We're giving away a FREE TABLET to one lucky household
To enter for the prize follow these steps:

1) Like our page
2) Tag 3 friends below who are also going through homeschooling just like you!

3) Share this post!

Good luck everyone!

We will announce the winner in one week"

We used an image of a tablet and branded it with the client's logo and colours.

We then shared a reminder 3 more times that week before announcing the winner.

Whilst people were tagging, sharing, and commenting, I was adding the new names to the client's network by sending friend requests and thank you messages to further engage with the new connections.

Once we finally announced the winner, in the post itself we tagged the lucky winner and then they also did a post on their feed tagging the broker back.

This allowed the broker to increase their following with at

least 100 more connections, not to mention, thousands of views.

Don't forget to have some fun. Sometimes the post doesn't have an agenda other than to have a laugh.

Awareness is awareness right? Whether you see my content and smile, or you see my content and buy, it's still awareness.

Take this for example:

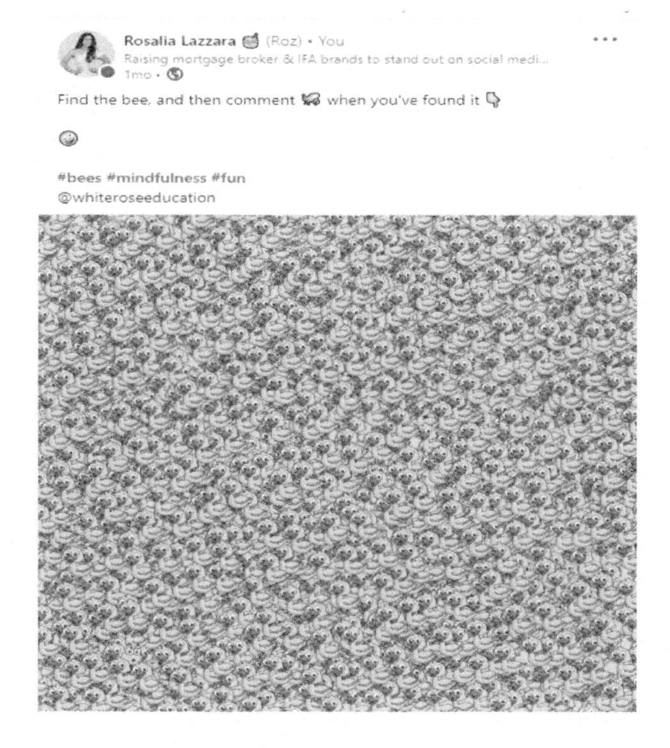

One Friday I posted this little mindfulness game. You have to find the bee (brand related) amongst the ducks.

Not only did I get over 3,000 views and 18 comments within a matter of hours, but I also got 16 private messages!!!

16 private 1 to 1 messages from, you guessed it, financial advisers and mortgage brokers, telling me they enjoyed it and thanked me for making them smile.

No, I didn't proceed to pitch to them, but they are in my inbox! They are engaged. They are enjoying following me.

This shows the importance of having content that is pleasant and welcoming. You don't want to always educate, sell, or inform. Sometimes you just want to share something positive and uplifting.

4. **Posting and Ghosting**

Avoid at all costs posting on social media and immediately logging off.

If all you ever do is post, then your numbers will not change and your results will not improve.

Posting on social media and logging off waiting for the leads to pour in, is like going to a networking event, throwing hundreds of business cards in the air, walking out, and expecting people to pick them up off the floor and calling you for business.

When you post on social media, make sure you allocate time in your calendar to engage with people!

I do a couple of different things with my clients whose social media profile I manage:

a) Either we post AND engage with followers and prospects on their behalf
b) We post and the client does the engagement

Either way, someone has to do the engagement.

The best combination is option A with the additional engagement personally done by the client themselves too. This adds to the activity and helps the account grow faster but if the client really hasn't got time then we try to do as much as the heavy lifting as possible. However, at least 10% of the month's engagement activity should come from you because you personally know people and connections that the social media manager wouldn't.

If you do have a social media manager or an administrator doing the posting and engagement for you, then be sure to at least check in a few times a month to specifically engage with people you know i.e clients, friends, and family.

Whilst the social media manager can engage with NEW prospects and introducers, only you can truly make a message personal with the people you already know.

It only takes a couple of minutes per day to send a meaningful message to an existing contact. Show them you're thinking of them.

Try this: the next time someone likes your post, send them a thank you message. Tell them that you appreciate their engagement and that you're happy that they are enjoying your content. See where the conversation takes you

Here are examples of how well this has been working for me and how impactful it can be on the relationship you're building your audience:

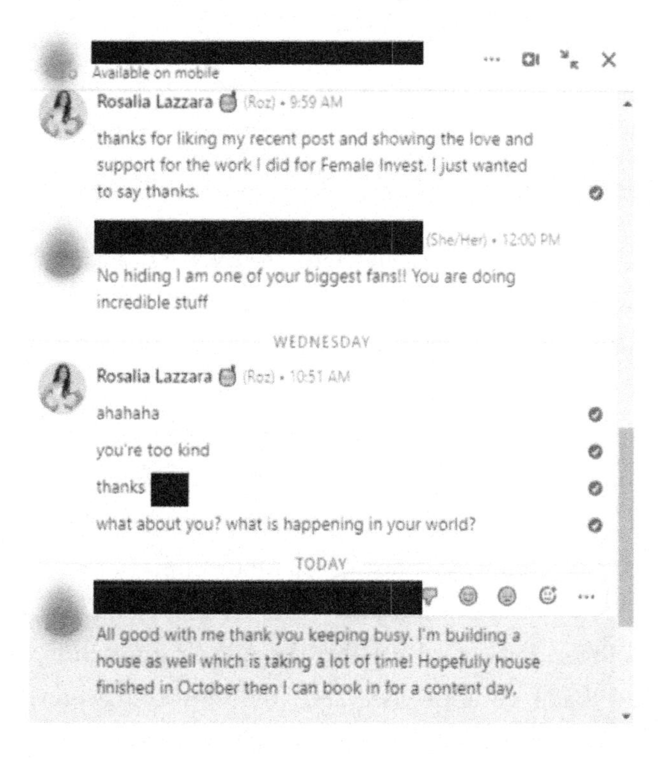

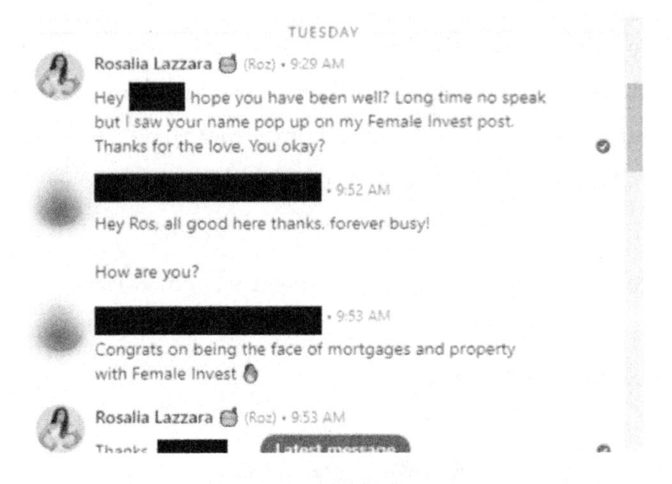

You don't get a message from Richard Branson saying "thanks for liking my post" right?

This is what I love about being where I am at. Small but known. Still close enough to my business and my connections to personally show them I care.

Fame for the sake of fame is not my goal. I'm not trying to be famous, BUT the more people that know me, the more people I can serve. This is how I care for my followers and how I try to have meaningful connections with them.

I apologise if I can't keep this up in the future. But please know that I do appreciate and value my connections and followers. I hope my content and work touches your heart in other ways and leaves a positive lasting impression even if I may not see it.

5. Being a trend junkie

If you find yourself jumping on every trend, you will dilute the message of your channel. Many people jump on all the dance, miming, audio, and other visual trends purely for the sake of getting as many views as quickly as possible which links back to Vanity Metrics.

Doing trends might seem fun, but if they are not relevant to your message or brand, then it can actually be detrimental to the appearance of your brand.

Some trends can make you look different to what you actually want to achieve i.e the joker. If being "the comedian" or "the joker" is not your style, then don't do it. You might enjoy the views for a little while but I promise it won't last long.

Absolutely do keep an eye out for trends particularly trending audios or songs that you can apply to your own business message. These are great fun and make your message stick.

Why do you think big brands on TV adverts pay thousands for the rights to a tune? The catchier the tune the more memorable the advert. I am sure you can sing in your head the Coca Cola advert, GoCompare, or Comparethemarket.com adverts?

Select the trends carefully and make sure they match your brand.

Let me talk to you about the time when I first started my TikTok account.

It was March 2020 and I was on furlough. The world was on lockdown. I had nothing to do. I thought my furlough would last 3 weeks and then I would be back to my job so I decided to have some "short term" fun. I discovered TikTok and decided to start trying out the trends.

Being a dancer, it felt natural to me to try out all the dance routines.

3 weeks turned into 3 months…

Not only was it a great workout, I managed to suddenly get 10k followers in 12 weeks.

The numbers didn't mean very much to me because a) I needed to go back to work b) I had no intentions or plans with these followers. I was just on the platform for self expression and enjoyment.

Once I actually did decide to start my own business in August 2020, I realised that actually, the following I had on TikTok wasn't going to be relevant so I decided to build a strategy on LinkedIn where I knew most of my ideal customers would be present.

Others would have potentially taken a different approach. They would have seen 10k followers on their account and think *"I will change the name to a business name and now start selling my services to these random people"*

There's no point using a high following with the wrong message. Those followers I had gained were due to my dancing! Their interest was in me as a dancer. I had women commenting on how inspired they felt and others commenting on my looks… Let's not go there.

Had I started a business selling dance apparel, then yes it would have made sense to sell these items on this existing account because the followers could potentially be interested in buying dance related items.

Instead I started a digital marketing business for financial advisers so I had to find the right content and platform for THEM.

Make sure the trends you're jumping on are relevant to your audience!

Here's how I created my own trend to make it relatable to my audience.

By September 2020 my audience knew that I had been made redundant and was starting my own business. Everyone shared with me how brave I was being and congratulated me on my journey.

We were all, as a nation, going through turbulent times. With homeworking, homeschooling, reduced incomes, high workloads, and dying high streets, our compassion and empathy for one another grew.

Our craving for connectivity grew further, giving us no option but to cling on to video calls and social media interaction.

It is for this reason that with no agenda or much thinking around what I was doing, I decided to post a picture of my workspace.

My workspace at the time being…. The ironing board! I was using the ironing board as my desk because my husband, also working from home, took up the spare bedroom.

This went viral.

Soon you started to see other people within my network doing the same. People reached out to me to tell me how amused they were. I even landed a big mortgage and wealth network deal off the back of it. The network principal got in touch and literally said and I quote: *"You're a nutter, let's work together"*.

People knew how hard it must have been as a brand new business owner trying to overcome redundancy and lockdown whilst starting a business. That's why sharing the reality and the behind the scenes of the journey really helped my audience connect with me.

It wasn't a trend that made it global, but it was a trend relevant to my audience who could get to know the real me.

Do not be afraid of being yourself. That's the best version of you and the version people most love to connect with.

6. **Keyboard warriors**

You'd think it would be obvious but you'd be surprised. I have seen many "reputable" financial advisers who let themselves down because they let their guard down as a business professional and engaged in controversial and offensive commentary.

Unfortunately, some people who don't have a filter (get it ;)) can't resist. They become keyboard warriors and others react to abusive behaviour or get sucked in by trolls.

Let's dive into all things regarding trolling, offensive posts, controversial commentary etc.

Firstly, never ever get sucked in by trolls. Trolls are cyberbullies. They go out of their way to maliciously attack another social media user. If you live your life with the fear of trolls, you are not living at all and you have let them win. Trolls are hateful to anyone and everyone. There's no rationale or justification to their actions. It's evil and random but you need to rise above it.

I do appreciate that sometimes these comments can be hurtful, and damn right wrong. It's happened to me. I totally get how it feels. BUT they only matter if you give them importance. Being affected by them is exactly what makes the trolls win. The trolls survive off your misery. Don't give it to them. Don't give them that satisfaction.

Trolls aside, let's talk about your behaviour too.

Nobody likes to be trolled so don't be one either.

Again, it may seem surprising to you, but I have seen people (even at senior level) in the financial services industry publicly declare their absurd views or put down others. They don't do this anonymously either. These people I refer to as people without a filter, are sometimes seen commenting trash on other people's posts, belittling either their competitors, or even being passive aggressive.

Being offensive in general is sad, but to plaster it on social media for everyone to see is going to be deadly for your brand and connections.

Controversy sells. Trust me, some "controversial" statements and posts are technically acceptable on social media and don't cross the line but make enough of a statement to call people's attention. The key is not to cross that line with homophobic, racist, misogynistic or otherwise hateful commentary.

What's the fine line?

Take Rob Moore for example. He's the founder of Progressive Property and a famous property tycoon. He's been very vocal about the pros and cons of the property world, sharing the brutal realities of running a business, and dispelling certain myths of the property game so that people don't make silly and costly mistakes. He's trying to protect his community from scammers and untrustworthy guidance online.

James Smith PT, famous for his sheer candidness and brutality. He does it with the cheekiest wit and humour. If you have not heard of him, check him out on Instagram. He basically takes fad diets and gimmick style workouts and rips them apart. He tells the viewer why not to follow this method, this diet etc. He does it with loving intentions deep down which is to remove the BS on social media around the fitness industry which is damaging to people's health.

Trump? Yeah maybe not.

7. **Lack of confidentiality**

Is social media unsafe? It is if you let it be.

In fact, social media can be very safe because you are protected by the screen. Nobody can get to you unless you let them. You are behind a screen and all that people can see is what you let them see.

Of course scammers and hackers are getting better and wiser these days. There are so many people who have tried to scam me by creating copycat profiles. They have pretended to be someone they are not!

Look out for things like this:

This is a typical scam message! They have copied another person's account, stolen their photos, bought followers and followed a bunch of people from the original account, and then messaged them to pretend to have an educational programme for how to generate multiple sources of income. They pretend to engage in conversation because they try to sell you something illegitimate.

Don't overshare where you are, where you live, your car details, your mother's maiden name, your favourite pet name from your childhood etc. When taking photos check your surroundings. Don't accept to meet strangers even if the opportunity seems juicy.

Don't do all the obvious things you would advise your child not to do!

IF YOU CANNOT DO GREAT THINGS, DO SMALL THINGS IN A GREAT WAY

— Napoleon Hill

Chapter Eight: Setting Up Your Content Calendar, And Scheduling

In this chapter, we explore the foundations of content planning, equipping you with the tools to take control of your digital narrative.

A well-structured content calendar provides organisation and boosts productivity. It serves as your compass, ensuring consistent engagement with your audience.

In the latter part of this chapter, we focus on strategic scheduling. Timing becomes the catalyst for success as we explore the intricacies of reaching your target audience effectively. We also discuss automation tools and flexibility, empowering you to adapt and thrive in a dynamic digital landscape.

It's all about time management and being organised so let's dive in.

Content calendar setup

A content calendar, also known as an editorial calendar, is a planning tool that helps individuals or businesses organise and schedule their content creation and distribution activities.

It provides a visual overview of planned content, including topics, formats, and publication dates, allowing for a structured and strategic approach to content creation.

A content calendar ensures that the right content is produced and shared at the right time. It helps maintain consistency, manage resources effectively, and align content with overarching goals and target audience preferences.

By outlining content themes, deadlines, and distribution channels, a content calendar enables individuals or teams to streamline their content production process, maintain a consistent publishing schedule, and maximise the impact of their content marketing efforts.

But how do you set one up?

Setting up a content calendar involves several steps to ensure it aligns with your goals, audience, and content strategy.

Here's a general guide on how to set up a content calendar:

1. Define your goals: Start by clarifying your content marketing goals. Are you aiming to increase brand awareness, drive website traffic, generate leads, or engage your audience? Understanding your objectives will shape your content calendar strategy.

2. Identify your target audience: Determine who your content is intended for. Research their demographics, interests, and pain points. This information will help you create content that resonates with your audience.

3. Choose a format and frequency: Decide on the types of content you want to create, such as blog posts, videos, podcasts, or social media posts. Consider your available resources and the preferences of your target audience. Determine how often you'll publish content—whether it's daily, weekly, or monthly.

4. Generate content ideas: Brainstorm topics that align with your goals and audience interests. Consider conducting keyword research, browsing industry forums, and analysing competitors to identify popular and relevant content ideas.

5. Create a content calendar template: Use a spreadsheet, calendar tool, or specialised content management software to create your content calendar template. Include columns for content titles, formats, assigned authors, publication dates, and distribution channels.

6. Plan content themes and topics: Organise your content calendar by themes or categories that align with your overall content strategy. Assign topics or keywords to specific dates to maintain a consistent flow of content.

7. Assign responsibilities: Assign team members or authors to specific content pieces. Clearly communicate deadlines and expectations for each piece of content.

8. Add distribution channels: Identify the platforms and channels where you will publish and promote your content. This can include your website blog, social media platforms, email newsletters, or third-party publications. Assign appropriate channels for each content piece in your calendar.

9. Review and refine: Regularly review and update your content calendar. Monitor content performance, audience engagement, and industry trends. Use this feedback to refine your future content planning and optimise your content strategy.

10. Adapt and be flexible: Remain flexible to accommodate unforeseen events, industry news, or changes in your business priorities. Adjust your content calendar accordingly, but strive to maintain consistency and stay on track with your overall content goals.

Remember, setting up a content calendar is an ongoing process. Continuously evaluate and refine your approach based on the feedback and results you receive, ensuring that your content calendar remains a dynamic and effective tool for your content marketing efforts.

Planning your ideas for the content calendar

I have given you the 7 Pillars to inspire you to generate as many content ideas as possible. Now you have to decide WHEN you are going to post them. Before diving into your 7 content pillars I want you to take 3 simple steps first.

What I do with my content schedule and my clients' is to have a meeting at the beginning of each month to map out the plan ahead. Whether you're alone or you have internal/outsourced support, this meeting at the beginning of each month is crucial to ensure you stay on track.

1. The first thing we do is to review the previous month. What worked and what didn't? We look at the best performing posts and the least engaging posts before we decide what is going to work in the next schedule. Once we have picked the best performing posts we brainstorm how we can repeat this level of success or make it even better. We look at the times in which we posted, the days, the copy and the imagery. We try to replicate the message without copying. We don't want our audience to see the same post over and over again.

If you are new to posting and you haven't posted before then jump to point number 2.

2. Have a look at this month's calendar to see what is happening in the diary. We take stock of all the meetings coming up, the events, the personal engagements etc.

Is there a team member's birthday coming up? We add it to the content calendar to wish them a happy birthday.

Is there an industry event that you're attending? Is it worth letting your audience know that you will be there?

Do you have important meetings in the diary with lenders? Perhaps your audience would benefit from knowing that you are going to be speaking to decision makers to help their mortgage application move forward.

Are you going to a networking event? Perhaps you could share the lessons and the highlights from your meeting.

The diary is often a great content idea generation tool. Work out what you need to share with your audience based on the tasks and events going on in your diary.

3. Name days. Is it pancake day for example?

Have a look at the yearly calendar to see what RELEVANT name days you need to know about.

Everyone posts on pancake day, but what does that mean for you?

If you too post your pancake with Nutella and strawberries it's going to go unnoticed because everyone is doing the same on the same day. Our feeds get clogged up with sugary recipes and we become indifferent to the same post being overshared.

How can you be different?

Is it Pride Month? Perhaps you can share how your business is embracing inclusivity and diversity.

On World Cancer day you could take part in a fundraising charitable cause, or volunteer. Share your experiences on this subject.

Name days are a great way to honour the things important to us. They are not there just to tick a box. They are designed to honour and remember important people, events, and situations in the world.

These name days are great for marketing. The content you post, gives us an insight into your values and helps you to connect more with your audience.

You want to create weekly, monthly, and quarterly focus strategies to avoid posting random content at any given time.

Remember, no two months are the same and the content must reflect this. You don't want to keep posting the same thing over and over again.

If you check out manukamedia.co.uk/socialmediaguide you will find another gift in there for you. There is a free 30-day content calendar. I have mapped out a 30-day plan for you to adopt. It's worthwhile trying if:

1. You haven't posted in a while and feel a bit rusty.
2. Never posted and want to start practising.
3. Need to try new ideas and diversify your own content.

Remember these ideas are generic. They are not specific to you or to the month you start. They are purely suggestions ready to be put into action but you still have to create the content.

Scheduling

Even for us content creators, scheduling can be a very time-consuming task.

I imagine that the biggest thing you struggle with on a daily basis is finding the time to post content, right?

You do not need to post content daily by logging in daily and manually uploading it. It would be a waste of time, even for full time social media managers.

The best way is to schedule in advance.

This way, you never miss the optimal time to post and you don't have to fit it into your daily tasks leaving you free to get on with your day job of course.

Scheduling should be done either weekly or monthly.

First step is to create the content in bulk. Write your week's post in advance so that you have your whole week mapped out. Secondly, get your graphics ready such as photos, videos, or other imagery you want to use with your copy. Thirdly, pick a scheduling tool that helps you to upload the post across multiple platforms if that's what you plan to do in your strategy.

Once your posts are scheduled for the week, you can simply focus on engagement! Scheduling your posts in advance gives you the freedom to focus on daily engagement and growing your following.

Quick hack: 30 minutes before your post is scheduled to go out, engage with your audience and quickly comment on 10 people's posts! This helps bump up the engagement on your own post when it's due to come out because people would have already been engaging with you on their post and are more likely to repay the favour. It's a little trick that the algorithm favours. It pushes the content to more people, especially the ones you have been recently engaging with.

CONTENT IS ANYTHING
THAT ADDS VALUE TO
A READERS'S LIFE.
— Avinash Kaushik

Chapter Nine: To Outsource Or Not To Outsource

Your decision to outsource or not comes down to:

1) Time
2) Budget
3) Skills

Outsourcing can enable you to free up your time and dedicate it to more crucial tasks at hand that you cannot outsource, for example: giving personal finance advice to your clients.

If you get paid to give advice, then 80% of your time should be invested in this. Do not get distracted by Canva posts and video editing.

Before making that decision, have a look at the 3 choices available when it comes to implementing your social media and content marketing campaign:

1. Self learn and figure it out along the way.
2. Get proper training and develop the skills necessary.
3. Outsource it, and hand it over to someone who's an expert.

What's for sure is that you need a plan. Winging it in today's world won't cut it because social media has been around for 20+ years. It's not new anymore.

Even though you're new to the social media scene, you still have to meet today's standards and trends.

To quote one of my favourite Money Honeys out there, *"Everything is figure-outable"* - Marie Forleo.

In case you're wondering what "Money Honey" is all about, it's related to my podcast The Money Honey which is a show bringing together women in finance, construction and property. You should check it out on Spotify if you haven't already.

In this chapter we delve into the critical question faced by businesses: "To outsource or not to outsource social media and content creation?". We will explore the advantages and disadvantages of both approaches, shedding light on the factors that should be considered before making a decision.

Income Producing Activity Vs. Traffic Producing Activity

In the realm of social media and content creation, businesses must distinguish between income producing activity and traffic producing activity. If you remember in chapter 5, I touched upon this briefly and I promised I would return to it. Income producing activity directly generates revenue through lead generation, sales conversions, and customer acquisition. On the other hand, traffic producing activity focuses on increasing brand visibility and engaging a wider audience. While income producing activity often benefits from an in-house approach, traffic producing activity can be outsourced to leverage specialised expertise. Striking the right balance between these activities is crucial for optimal revenue generation and brand growth.

I always say this to new prospective clients: there are two ways to pay. Two acceptable currencies. You can either pay with TIME or MONEY. Either way you have to pay to play.

You have to make a decision whether you choose to either invest your time prolifically to work on your social media strategy, or you pay someone to help you or do it for you.

As a business owner myself, here is the question I ask myself daily and one that I will lend to you because it's a question you should ask yourself too: *Will my time spent doing this task bring in money, or cost me money?*

As a business owner, you're responsible for generating income and growing the business. Even if you don't want to scale your business to a large level, you still go to bed at night thinking about "where is the next client coming from?" Am I right?

That's why you have to be very diligent when it comes to IPA - Income Producing Activity.

No doubt, you are busy! I am sure you're juggling client appointments, reports, lender systems, market updates, navigating lender changes and product updates, as well as staff issues, legal matters, and personal problems too.

If you're not self-employed you might have other challenges at play but either way, you will still need to hit targets as an employee which comes down to IPA.

Traffic Producing Activity on the other hand is more about brand awareness.

Meeting with a new potential client = IPA
Engaging with audience online = TPA

Follow up call with an existing client = IPA
Posting content = TPA.

You get the idea.

Now it's your turn. Make a list of the tasks and responsibilities on your desk. Make a list of all the things you need to do. Next to each item I want you to write IPA or TPA.

This is how you decide what to keep and what to delegate.

It's impossible to do it all by yourself. Trying to make 12 mortgage applications, whilst responding to 25 emails, and posting 27 times per month is not realistic.

You need to concentrate on IPA whilst outsourcing the TPA.

If you find yourself on Canva for 3 hours, you are losing money, not making money!

If you have 1 hour, 3 hours, or 30 minutes spare, you should be investing that into IPA:

- Find a new client from your phone book you can call back and reignite a conversation.
- Follow up on the potential prospects from 3 months ago. Check in.
- Go to a networking event to drive more connections and partnerships.
- Ring an existing client and ask them if they have recently heard about someone who needs help with their mortgage/pension/investments.
- Ring an introducer and take them out for lunch.
- Text a colleague and see if they need any help. Perhaps they are too busy and need you to take some business off their hands?
- Ring a family member and see if they will introduce you to someone at work?

- Go to your local community, see if you can be of help and make some new connections.
- Ask your estate agent in town if they need a mortgage adviser to help.
- Sit in your local coffee shop and strike up a conversation.
- Ask the local businesses to get together for networking drinks.
- Host a webinar for your audience. Invite them to learn more about what you do.

All of the ideas above fall into IPA. This activity should well and truly stay within your area of responsibility.

Conversely, I have made a list below of the tasks that should be given to your DIGITAL admin support either in house or outsourced.

- Creating templates on Canva
- Editing videos
- Scheduling content
- Setting up an email campaign
- Building landing pages
- Creating a lead magnet
- Managing Facebook ads
- Adding copy to the website
- Managing funnels
- Engaging with audience on socials

By all means, learn about them, play with these tasks for a VERY short period of time to get to grips with them, but do not keep them on your to do list.

They will burn away time or not even get done at all.

Often when you try to do all things for the sake of saving a bob or two, it ends up costing you more in the long run. So let's explore that further.

I want to share with you how I got this lead on Instagram off the back of a party I attended. Rather than spending time creating Canva posts, I went out there to meet real people! Yes it cost me the train fare and hotel, but I was treated to free drinks, food, and a room full of potential clients and collaborators all night.

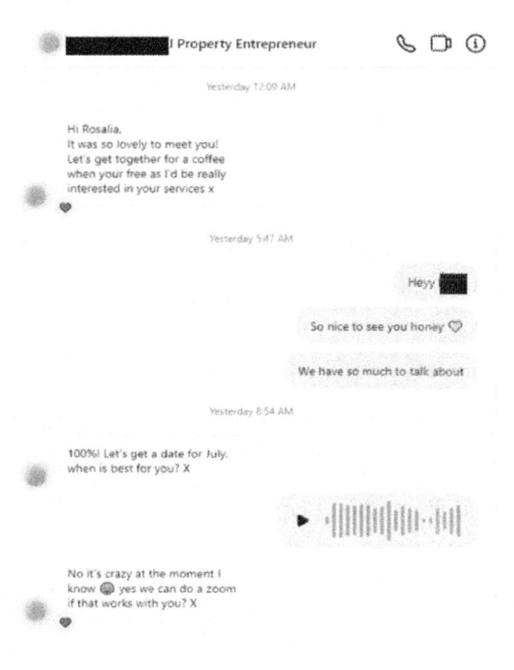

I went to a property networking event. It was invite only. Guess how and where I got invited?

Instagram!

At the time of being invited to this event, I only had 700 followers. At the event I met some celebs of the property world who have 10k+ followers and who I have been following for a while. This backs up my point that it's not about quantity but quality.

<u>Prior</u> to the event, I was engaging with people who were also big in the property space. Influencers such as podcasters, developers, and other professionals within property.

<u>During</u> the event, I introduced myself to those people I recognised from Instagram AND people were coming up to me too saying "loving the yellow" or "love what you're doing with financial education in schools" "love what you're doing with Money Honey podcast, I would love to be a guest". During the event we took selfies and added each other on Instagram. No, we didn't exchange business cards. How awkward. We just added each other directly on Instagram!

<u>Post event</u>: we started to tag each other in the posts. We documented the evening on our own profiles and tagged the people who featured in it. We tagged the event organiser too who reshared out posts. I commented on people's posts like this:

This helps keep the event and the energy alive!

Events and networking have 3 stages: Pre, During, and Post.

Notice how I did a bit of leg work BEFORE the event, during, and then after.

The event was still buzzing a week later. People followed up and connected because they remembered me from the party.

You don't do business at the event. It happens later.

As you can see from the lead I shared, I had a great evening with a new person I'd never met before and once we connected, she then expressed an interest in my services. I noticed she was looking at my profile and the content clearly explains what I do. This is how content can help you sell yourself without having to do it manually via telephone, email and text. The person who made an enquiry already did their research through my content and decided for themselves that they were interested. All I have to do is call them and discuss the next steps.

The Pros and Cons of Outsourcing

Here, we present a balanced exploration of the advantages and disadvantages associated with outsourcing social media management and content creation. On one hand, outsourcing can offer cost savings, access to specialised expertise, and enhanced scalability. On the other hand, it may result in reduced control over the brand's voice, potential misalignment with organisational values, and the risk of diluted authenticity if you are not working with the correct agency. We will delve into these pros and cons, highlighting real-life case studies to provide practical insights.

Firstly, if you are running large scale social media campaigns, and producing a prolific amount of content, then it might end up being more cost effective to hire someone in house or a freelancer on a retainer basis. It's great to have someone at your fingertips whenever you need them, but it's a costly overhead in your business.

Chances are, you don't need reams and reams of long form content and large-scale marketing campaigns, therefore it might be worth finding a freelance social media manager. It keeps the costs lower in comparison to hiring a full-time member of staff, but you will have to share them with someone else as they typically have multiple clients and their time is split.

The good news is that if they are a freelancer or a business owner, they tend to have more experience, be more independent, and can be very solution focused therefore won't require you to hold their hand.

The final option is hiring an apprentice. You can hire a young individual who needs experience whilst you are also making a positive impact in shaping their future. They learn and grow with your business.

However, they do not have experience. They will need a lot of guidance and handholding which could take up a lot of your time. If they don't know what to do they may require an external trainer or a consultant to bring them up to speed. You could also enrol them into a course and upskill them.

Deciding WHO you are going to be working with is crucial to getting set up for success.

However, outsourcing does not mean you hand it over entirely to a stranger and you personally free yourself from all responsibilities.

It's YOUR business. It's your brand. If you don't talk about your business, who will?

The outsourcing model is there to support, and enhance your existing business. It's not to replace you and remove you from the picture.

As a business owner, it is in your best interest to manage and oversee the marketing consultant, social media manager or content creator.

Outsourcing can sometimes lose the personal touch. If you're not careful in choosing the right company to work with, the external consultants or agencies may not be able to keep your voice integral to the brand and it could turn a bit generic.

Finding the right balance between outsourcing and in-house tasks is the key to working on what you do best and let the professionals handle the rest.

In conclusion the decision is down to your specific requirements, your circumstances and cashflow. Here's a summary of the points to consider:

Pros of Outsourcing:

1. Cost savings: Outsourcing can often be more cost-effective than maintaining an in-house team. It eliminates the need for hiring full-time employees and permanent overheads.

2. Access to specialised expertise: Outsourcing allows businesses to tap into the expertise of professionals who specialise in social media management and content creation. These experts have in-depth knowledge of the latest trends, best practices, and strategies to maximise engagement and reach.
3. Scalability: Outsourcing offers the flexibility to scale up or down based on the business's needs. During peak periods or when launching new campaigns, outsourcing allows for quick and efficient ramp-up of resources without the constraints of hiring and training new employees.

Cons of Outsourcing:

1. Reduced control over brand voice: When outsourcing social media and content creation, there is a risk of diluting the brand's voice and messaging. External agencies or individuals may not have the same level of familiarity with the brand's values and tone, potentially leading to inconsistencies.
2. Misalignment with organisational values: Outsourced providers may not fully understand or align with the business's core values and goals. This misalignment can result in content that does not resonate with the target audience or accurately represent the brand.
3. Potential loss of authenticity: Authenticity is highly valued by today's consumers. When content creation is outsourced, there is a risk of losing the genuine, personal touch that resonates with audiences. Authenticity plays a

crucial role in building trust and long-term customer relationships.

Chapter Ten: Organic Lead Generation Tactics

You're probably itching to complete this chapter on lead generation once and for all. I know the wait will have been worth it so I won't keep you waiting any longer.

While paid advertising on social media platforms can yield immediate results (if done properly), organic lead generation tactics on social media provide a sustainable and cost-effective approach to cultivating a loyal customer base.

We're not going to dive into paid advertising in this book. Assuming you are a novice on social media, paid advertising is not where you want to start.

Before blowing your budget on paying for ads, we are best off starting with building organic traction first and testing your early content on your existing audience for free.

Once you are more confident and you have a proven concept that the strategy is working, you can scale up with paid advertising.

To excel in lead generation, it's crucial to diversify your efforts and engage in a range of activities. These can include but are not limited to targeted advertising campaigns, content creation, social media engagement, email marketing, networking events, search engine optimization, and strategic partnerships. By incorporating these various tactics into your lead generation strategy, you broaden your reach, capture the attention of diverse audiences, and maximise your chances of success.

Chapter 10 delves into the realm of organic lead generation tactics specifically relating to social media. We will explore strategies that attract, engage, and convert potential customers. By understanding and implementing these tactics effectively, businesses can create a strong social media presence, increase brand visibility, and drive meaningful interactions that result in valuable leads.

I have already been building into the book many of these tactics and methods. You will have come across some already such as creating captivating content, engaging with your audience, and developing campaigns that are specific to your target audience, as well as real life networking on and offline.

There's still some more exciting tactics up my sleeve that I want to share that will help fill up your diary such as tapping into groups, communities, and collaborations with other influencers.

Caveat: All my tactics have been tried and tested on my own business and my clients. They don't always work out in the exact same way for everybody. There are no guaranteed results but I am confident enough to say that these have never failed me or my clients in some shape or form.

2nd caveat: I am teaching you the tactics I know TODAY. By the time I finish this book I may have already discovered some more which didn't quite make it into the book.

3rd Caveat: I am human. I may have forgotten one or two but if they didn't make it in they couldn't have been that important. I am sharing the ones I use daily and ones that yield the best results.

What this chapter will NOT teach you:

I will not be sharing immoral tactics. I have seen people create fake accounts and recommend a broker, or tag a broker when really they are tagging themselves. It's untruthful and not sustainable. If you have to create a fake account to tag yourself in the comments as a recommendation, then you don't really have a loyal customer base.

I've seen people name and shame certain businesses in the hope that they will get chosen for the job instead. Speaking ill of other businesses doesn't make you look any better. That is not a lead gen tactic.

As I dive into the top 16 tips, I am going to assume it is obvious that you:

A) Need to be consistent not only with your brand message and niche but also with the volume of posting.

B) Need to be creating captivating content relevant to your ideal customer.

1. It's a numbers game AND a quality game. The more people see your profile and content, the more likely you are to find your next customer. I will reword that to: "The more *relevant* people see your profile the more likely you are to find your next customer".

   If you only have 200 connections but you are writing stellar content, the conversion or number of leads you are expecting to see versus what you actually get might not be that high. Whilst I did say you do not need to be famous on social media to be successful, you do always need to keep expanding your network so that more people "walk into the store" so to speak.

   The more people see your content the more chances you have of finding the right customer.

   Keep adding new people to your network. Make sure you monitor how your following is growing.

2. As you see your following expand, keep up with the relationships. As I have mentioned before, make sure you make a meaningful connection with all of the new followers. Get into the habit of thanking everyone who follows you. Make it a habit to start the conversation even just by saying hello. You never know where the conversation might go.

Just by sending a "Merry Christmas and Happy New Year" message to an existing connection, this is the response I got back:

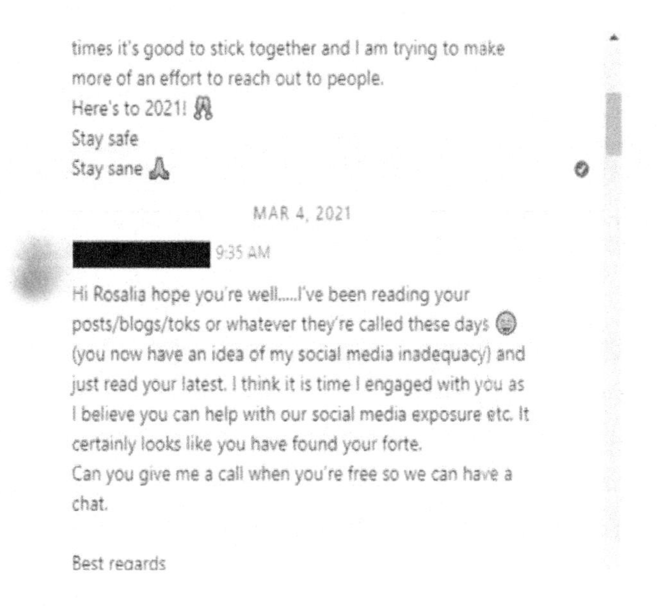

Whilst they didn't respond to my message at Christmas, they never forgot me and actually when they needed help, they came straight to me.

I'll never know why they didn't say Merry Christmas back to me, but I didn't take it personally. I didn't let that stop me from doing business with them later down the road.

Sometimes we open a message and think about returning to it later to respond but we just simply forget which is why you shouldn't get hung up about it. Keep persevering with your content and let people come to you when they are ready.

3. When someone likes your content and they happen to be an ideal customer who perhaps you've not engaged with before or haven't spoken to for a while, send them a private message and tell them you appreciate them liking your post. I have shared this one before and I will mention it again because it really has produced a lot of business for me and my clients.

   In an earlier chapter, I shared an example of how this method has helped me spark a conversation with people who follow me.

   It really goes a long way and it develops the 4-11-7 rule we discussed earlier too.

4. Comment on other people's posts and start a meaningful thread. This tactic doesn't generate much business for people if their comments are very vague and generic such as "thanks for sharing" or "nice post". It doesn't keep the conversation flowing. Don't get me wrong, sometimes that's all you can say and I also do it. But I encourage you whenever possible, at least 2 or 3 times per day, to try to share messages such as the one in the example below, because it really helps you stand out from the crowd and positions you as a thought leader.

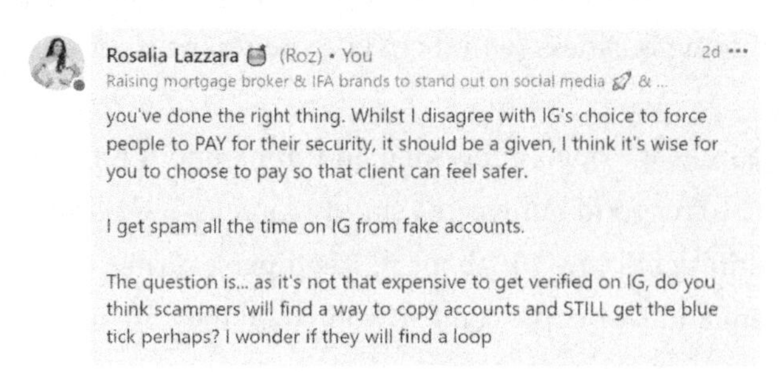

5. Building on top tip number 4, I recommend you instigate a conversation thread on your own posts. Tag people on your post who could add their comments or feedback. Perhaps you can instigate a conversation with one of your followers to say *"I would love to hear from XYZ and their expert opinion on ....".* Always apply my rule of "no spamming" to these things. You don't want to unnecessarily tag people who don't often engage with you or who have heard from you way too much. Try and apply common sense to this without damaging your relationship. Some people get tagged in a post that is irrelevant to them. They have only been tagged for the obvious reason that the content creator simply wants to get them to engage and to get more viewers on their post. This can be annoying because it's very transparent that you're doing it to gain more traction.

6. Join groups and communities on Facebook and LinkedIn that are in keeping with your niche. For example, one of my clients' ideal customers is self-employed people in construction so we added him to the LinkedIn group called Construction Who's Who. When a post or announcement goes out there, he has an alert to ensure he doesn't miss the conversation. He also tries to instigate a conversation there or share valuable information his customers might be interested in learning more about.

   Is there a group within your niche that you could be a part of? Perhaps your target audience is "mums in business" or "locum doctor". Type keywords into the search engines built within the social media platforms and see what you can find.

In this situation, if I were to build a community for my client whose ideal customer is "mums in business" I would be searching for the following on Instagram, Facebook and LinkedIn:

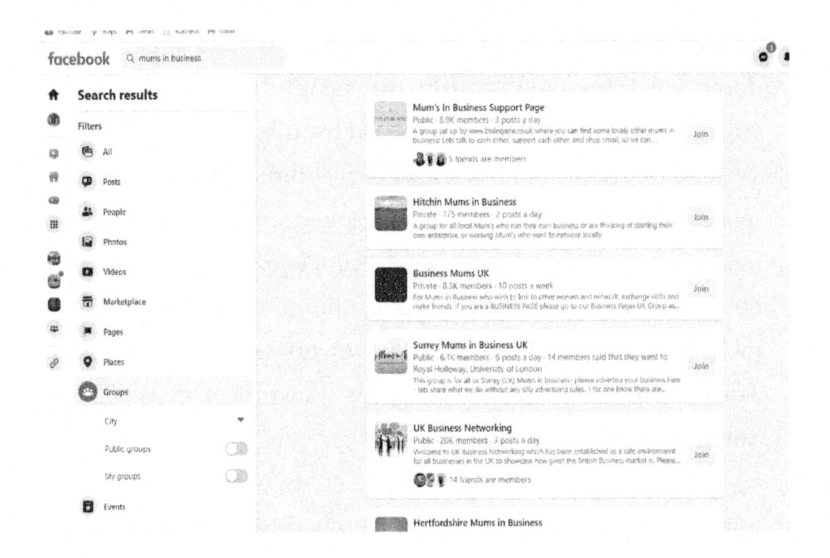

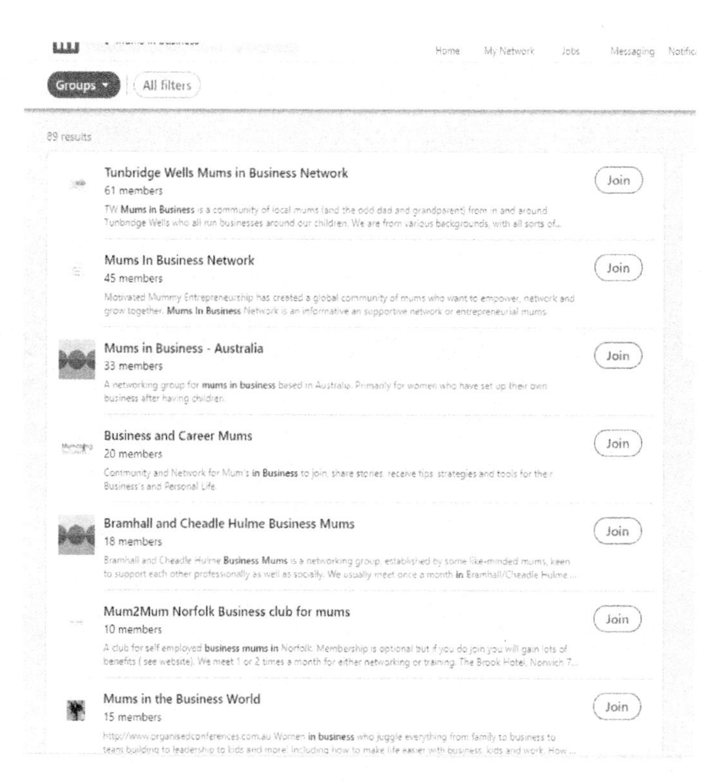
Home
My Network
Jobs
Messaging
Groups
All filters
89 results
Tunbridge Wells Mums in Business Network
61 members
TW Mums in Business is a community of local mums (and the odd dad and grandparent) from in and around Tunbridge Wells who all run businesses around our children. We are from various backgrounds, with all sorts of..
Join
Mums In Business Network
45 members
Motivated Mummy Entrepreneurship has created a global community of mums who want to empower, network and grow together. Mums In Business Network is an informative an supportive network or entrepreneurial mums.
Join
Mums in Business - Australia
33 members
A networking group for mums in business based in Australia. Primarily for women who have set up their own business after having children.
Join
Business and Career Mums
20 members
Community and Network for Mum's in Business to join, share stories, receive tips, strategies and tools for their Business's and Personal Life.
Join
Bramhall and Cheadle Hulme Business Mums
18 members
Bramhall and Cheadle Hulme Business Mums is a networking group, established by some like-minded mums, keen to support each other professionally as well as socially. We usually meet once a month in Bramhall/Cheadle Hulme ...
Join
Mum2Mum Norfolk Business club for mums
10 members
A club for self employed business mums in Norfolk. Membership is optional but if you do join you will gain lots of benefits (see website). We meet 1 or 2 times a month for either networking or training. The Brook Hotel, Norwich 7...
Join
Mums in the Business World
15 members
http://www.organisedconferences.com.au Women in business who juggle everything from family to business to team building to leadership to kids and more! Including how to make life easier with business, kids and work. How ...
Join

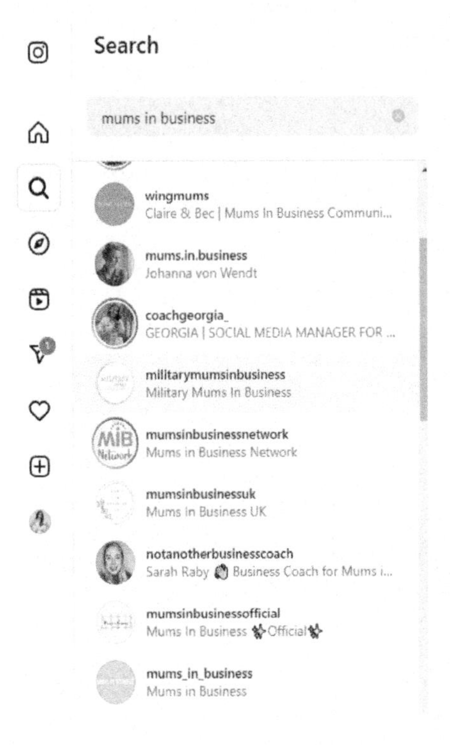

It all begins with a simple keyword search.

Find new groups, content, accounts, people, and events surrounding your niche.

7. Financial advisers and mortgage brokers always tell me that their best leads are referrals. Let's talk about DIGITAL recommendations and DIGITAL word of mouth. Particularly on Facebook, people ask for recommendations. *"I am looking for a gardener in Ely, can someone please recommend someone local?"*. Same goes for mortgages, pensions, investments, etc. If your friends and family would be so kind to tag you that would help your brand awareness and to get in front of people who are ready to buy. If you spot one of these

opportunities yourself, why not send it to your trusted friend and client and ask them to kindly tag you? I know it might seem cringy to you but sometimes your friends might not have seen it and actually would be more than happy to help you out! Getting online recommendations in public for everyone to see speaks volumes. People are always looking for good people and so when someone comes highly recommended and is visible on social media, they do well at winning the business.

8. If the group doesn't exist, make one! If you are trying to target Trades People in Essex, then perhaps you should start this group if one doesn't exist. Share helpful information, connect people, and network. This is a great way to meet new people. It's unlikely that some sort of group doesn't exist already, but in the case that it doesn't exist, make your own! Please also remember that the group might exist but it might not be active! If a group is inactive and doesn't engage the followers, there's no point joining the group. You want to find an engaging group that actively talks, meets, or shares information.

9. Appreciation posts. Just like when you ask your clients to leave you a review, ask them for an appreciation post. Something simple on social media to say *"Thanks Sam for sorting out our mortgage, you made the process super simple".* When your client posts about you, their network sees it too. People are curious so I guarantee they will be checking you out and who knows, they might need you too. This is a great opportunity to capitalise on this exposure. In the comments

section engage with the person who has posted this. Thank them back. Share your business page on the thread too. If your client has thanked you in public on their feed, when you respond saying "thankyou" in the comments section, add a quick note to plug in your business page such as *"thanks Sam, you were a joy to work with and I am so delighted you got the keys to your dream home. If anybody else needs mortgage help, please feel free to get in touch and check out @ABC Broker page"*. Then keep an eye out for other people who comment too or like the post. If you notice someone has the profile of your ideal customer avatar, and they have liked the post, add them!

10. Lead magnets. Give the people what they want in exchange for their email. We know that people aren't always ready to buy right away so you need to nurture the relationship and keep them in the funnel until they are ready to buy. When launching a lead magnet make sure you give the reader exactly what they want right away. Don't make them jump through hoops. If you have promised them an eBook, make sure that once their email address is submitted you have the eBook land in their inbox right away. Once they are in the Customer Relationship Management programme, then you can automate emails. Keep them up to date with your company news and helpful information.

11. Partnerships. A great way to get noticed by more potential customers is to partner up with someone who is aligned with your niche. For example, if your ideal customers are self-employed, perhaps you could partner with an accountant and create some content together that you can both share? Could

you do a guest blog for their newsletter and vice versa? Could you have some social media dual branded content?

12. Press features. Having your name in well-known publications helps to convert. Could you approach your local radio, newspaper, magazine to feature in a story? There's always plenty to talk about in the financial word so perhaps you could be a spokesperson for this.

13. Guest speaker on podcasts. These are hard to get invited to unless you already have some sort of online presence. The podcast hosts want interesting guests on their show and if you haven't built up a reputation on social media yet it might be hard to get asked to speak but you can certainly start working towards this. Don't sit and wait to be asked. Engage with podcast hosts, listen to their shows, engage with their speakers, and then send them a message to express your interest. Give them a story and a reason to invite you.

14. Freebies. a giveaway, if suitable to your brand, is always a great way to capture people's interest. They might not be ready to invest with you right away but if you give them a flavour of your service for free, it's a great way to get them into the funnel. Your content will naturally build up that picture in their minds. Hosting an event or a webinar can help your audience get to know you better.

15. Google reviews. These are free to give and free to use! It massively boosts your search ranking in Google and adds great value to your brand. Ask EVERYONE you work with to

give you a Google Review. Once potential customers search your name in Google, they want to instantly see that you are a brand they can trust.

16. Google My Business (GMB) helps with lead generation by increasing online visibility, providing contact information and website links, showcasing customer reviews, enabling messaging and booking, and offering insights on listing performance. By optimising your GMB profile, you attract more leads through local search results, engage potential customers, and build credibility, ultimately driving business growth.

Lead generation is not a single task but rather a culmination of various smaller activities carried out consistently over time, which collectively empower you to gain momentum. In essence, the purpose of this chapter extends beyond merely selecting a couple of activities that you personally prefer. It revolves around striking a harmonious balance among all the different tasks and executing them in synchrony to realise truly remarkable outcomes.

However, it is not enough to simply engage in these activities individually. The key lies in synchronising them, ensuring that they complement and reinforce one another.

So, rather than focusing on a few preferred activities, strive to create a symphony of lead generation strategies that work together to achieve your desired goals.

Chapter Eleven: Navigating Social Media Crises And Reputation Management For UK Mortgage Brokers

In the fast-paced world of social media, where information spreads like wildfire, even the most well-planned social media strategies can sometimes lead to unforeseen crisis. As a mortgage broker, it is essential to be prepared for potential social media crises and understand how to effectively manage your reputation online. Let's talk about reputation repair to help you safeguard your brand and maintain a positive online presence.

1. Anticipate Potential Risks

Before you dive into any social media campaign, it is crucial to conduct a thorough risk assessment. Identify potential hazards that could arise from your content, interactions, or external factors. Common risks for mortgage brokers may include misinformation, negative client experiences, regulatory issues, cloning and impersonation of accounts, or competitive attacks. Once you have identified potential risks, develop a crisis communication plan to address these scenarios promptly and efficiently.

2. Respond Quickly and Transparently

In the event of a social media crisis, time is of the essence. Your response must be swift and transparent. Acknowledge the issue, take responsibility, and offer reassurance to those affected. Avoid deleting negative comments or ignoring the problem, as this may exacerbate the situation and damage your reputation further. Instead, respond openly, apologise if necessary, and demonstrate your commitment to resolving the issue.

3. Stay Calm and Professional

A social media crisis can be emotionally charged, but it is essential to remain calm and composed in your responses. Avoid engaging in heated arguments or personal attacks. Responding with professionalism and empathy will show that you take the matter seriously and are committed to finding a resolution. Remember that your responses are public and can impact your reputation, so choose your words wisely.

4. Monitor and Listen

Monitoring social media conversations is vital to detect potential crises early on. Utilise social listening tools to stay on top of mentions, comments, and discussions related to your brand. By actively listening to your audience, you can address emerging issues promptly and prevent them from escalating into larger problems.

5. Empower Your Team

Ensure that your social media team is well-equipped to handle crisis situations. Establish clear protocols for crisis management and provide training on effective communication during challenging times. Empower your team to make decisions quickly and escalate issues to higher management if necessary.

6. Leverage Influencers and Advocates

During a crisis, having a strong network of influencers and brand advocates can be invaluable. Engage with influencers who align with your brand values and can vouch for your credibility. Their support and positive testimonials can help mitigate the impact of negative publicity and reaffirm your brand's trustworthiness.

7. Rebuild Trust

Rebuilding trust after a social media crisis is crucial. Demonstrate your commitment to learning from the experience and improving your services. Implement changes based on customer feedback and provide updates on progress regularly. Engaging in open dialogue with your audience will show that you value their opinions and are actively working to regain their trust.

As a mortgage broker, your reputation is one of your most valuable assets. Understanding how to navigate social media crises and effectively manage your online reputation is vital for long-term success. By being proactive, transparent, and empathetic in your communications, you can turn potential crises into opportunities to strengthen your brand and build lasting trust with your audience. Remember, crises are an inevitable part of the social media landscape, but with the right approach and preparedness, you can emerge stronger and more resilient than ever before.

CONTENT MARKETING IS THE ONLY MARKETING LEFT

— Seth Godin

Chapter Twelve: Staying Compliant and Ethical on Social Media

In the world of social media, where information flows freely and opinions are shared openly, maintaining compliance and ethical standards is paramount for mortgage brokers. As a professional in the financial industry, it is essential to navigate social media platforms while adhering to regulatory guidelines and ethical principles.

But are you stuck in analysis paralysis?

Many financial advisers have often stopped themselves from posting on social media or never even attempted it, frightened by what their compliance team might say. Some have actually been warned once or twice about "non compliant" content and asked to take it down. This does not stop them from carrying on.

I will make a bold enough statement to say that to this date none of my clients have been asked to take down their content. None of them have lost videos, articles, blogs, or any other form of content because there is a way!

1. Familiarise Yourself with Regulatory Requirements
As a mortgage broker, it is crucial to stay up-to-date with the regulatory requirements set forth by governing bodies such as the Financial Conduct Authority (FCA) in the UK.

Get familiar with the rules and guidelines specific to social media usage and advertising. Understand the limitations and restrictions surrounding promotional activities, disclosures, and client confidentiality. By having a solid understanding of the regulations, you can confidently navigate social media platforms while avoiding potential compliance pitfalls.

2. Develop a Social Media Policy

Create a comprehensive social media policy for your brokerage firm. This policy should outline the dos and don'ts of social media usage, addressing topics such as appropriate content, engagement with clients, disclosure of affiliations, and handling sensitive information. Ensure that all employees and representatives of your firm are aware of and trained in adhering to this policy. Regularly review and update the policy to accommodate any changes in regulations or social media platforms.

At this point, if you do decide to keep the content creation and social media management in house then professional training with a social media manager is always a good idea to help you formalise the process.

3. Exercise Discretion and Professionalism

When engaging on social media, maintain a professional demeanour at all times. Avoid making exaggerated claims, false promises, or engaging in unethical practices. Ensure that all content shared is accurate, honest, and relevant to your audience. Refrain from discussing confidential client information or engaging in negative or defamatory discussions. Remember, your online presence is a reflection of your professionalism and integrity as a mortgage broker.

4. Disclose Affiliations and Conflicts of Interest.

Transparency is key when disclosing affiliations and potential conflicts of interest on social media. If you are endorsing a product or service, make it clear that it is a paid partnership or an affiliate arrangement. Disclose any potential conflicts of interest that may arise from your engagements, ensuring that your audience understands your relationships and can make informed decisions based on the information you provide.

5. Be Mindful of Client Privacy and Data Protection

Respect client privacy and ensure that you adhere to data protection laws, such as the General Data Protection Regulation (GDPR). Obtain necessary consents when collecting client information and handle data securely. Avoid sharing sensitive client details on social media platforms, and be cautious about discussing specific cases or scenarios that may breach client confidentiality.

6. Monitor and Moderate User-Generated Content:

On social media, user-generated content, such as comments and reviews, can influence your reputation. Monitor and moderate these interactions to ensure compliance with your social media policy. Promptly address any inappropriate or misleading content, and foster a respectful and constructive dialogue with your audience. By actively managing user-generated content, you can maintain a positive online environment and protect your brand's reputation.

7. Seek Legal and Compliance Guidance

If you have any doubts or concerns regarding compliance and ethical practices on social media, seek legal counsel or consult with compliance experts. They can provide guidance specific to your brokerage firm and ensure that you are navigating social media platforms in a manner that aligns with industry regulations and ethical standards.

Staying compliant and ethical on social media is a fundamental responsibility for UK mortgage brokers. By familiarising yourself with regulatory requirements, developing a social media policy, exercising professionalism, and maintaining client confidentiality, you can establish a strong foundation for ethical conduct on social media. Remember, compliance and ethical practices should be integrated into every aspect of your social media presence. By upholding these standards and staying vigilant in your social media activities, you can build trust with your audience, protect your professional reputation, and ensure that you are providing accurate and reliable information to those seeking your services.

Conclusion

As we wrap up this incredible journey into the world of social media marketing for mortgage brokers, let's take a moment to reflect on the excitement that lies ahead. Throughout this book, we've delved into the boundless possibilities and remarkable impact that social media holds. But here's the deal: it's time to get cracking and make things happen!

Social media isn't just a passing fad; it's become an integral part of our lives. It's where we connect, share, and showcase our brand's accomplishments and mission. And guess what? As mortgage brokers, we've got a front-row seat to harness this digital powerhouse and propel our businesses to new heights! Now more than ever, society is faced with fast paced changes and difficult circumstances on the horizon so they need to know where you are and how you can help.

So, what's the hold-up? Why wait around? Let's spring into action! This book has shared the pure liquid gold on all the strategies, tips, and tricks you need to conquer the social media game. But here's the secret ingredient to the real honey: reading alone won't cut it! It's time to roll up our sleeves, jump into the digital playground, and put these golden nuggets of wisdom into practice.

That's where the real money is, honey.

You see, social media has the power to be a game-changer when used effectively. It's our ticket to connect with dream clients, establish ourselves as industry experts, and make a tangible difference in our businesses. But here's the catch: none of this will magically happen unless we take action. So, let's embrace the urgency, recognize the importance, and make a commitment right now to implement these activities like there's no tomorrow!

Remember, change only occurs when we make it happen. And when it comes to social media, the time to act is now. So, let's seize the opportunity, step boldly into the digital realm, and unleash the full potential of social media marketing for our mortgage broker businesses. The future is bright, but it's up to us to make it shine!

If we want to empower consumers to make sound financial decisions and improve their financial wellbeing, then we need to be the pioneers of that change and show them what is possible.

Social media is no overnight success. It certainly isn't waiting for you to come along and hand over a bunch of leads just because you posted your first video. It requires patience, perseverance, creativity, and consistency.

If you are ready to take this seriously then you will enter a scene where you could be rubbing shoulders with a property tycoon like Rob Moore, or a serial entrepreneur like Jeff Bezos. Entering the social media network puts you in the same room as Martin Lewis and even Greta Thunberg.

It's a FREE 24/7 live party, and you're invited.

How will you make your mark?

We invite you, if you haven't already, to follow Manuka Media on Instagram, subscribe to The Money Honey podcast on Spotify, and connect with Rosalia Lazzara on all social networks including Instagram, LinkedIn, Threads, and TikTok.

P.S. see what I did there?

I mentioned Threads!

By the time I got to the conclusion of this book a new platform came on the social media scene. A platform that wasn't around when I first started the book so I didn't include it in the chapters.

I purposely haven't gone back to add my teachings and findings on Threads because A) it just shows you how fast the social media scene can change at any moment and that you need to constantly adapt and adopt. You can't rely on the teachings from this book forever. You have to keep refreshing your knowledge and experience and constantly keep up to date. B) You'll have to stay tuned for the next book ;-) or go on my social media feed to find out the latest updates and comments I share about the current social networks.

CREATIVITY IS

INTELLIGENCE HAVING FUN

— Albert Einstein

References

Introduction:

Forbes. (2023). Top Social Media Statistics And Trends of 2023. Retrieved from https://www.forbes.com/advisor/business/social-media-statistics/#:~:text=In%202023%2C%20an%20estimated%204.9,5.85%20billion%20users%20by%202027

Chapter 1:

Exploding Topics. (2023). Amount of Data Created Daily (2023). Retrieved from https://explodingtopics.com/blog/data-generated-per-day

Chapter 2:

Ministry of Housing, Communities, & Local Government. (2021). English Housing Survey. Retrieved from https://assets.publishing.service.gov.uk/government/uploads/system/uploads/attachment_data/file/1000052/EHS_19-20_PRS_report.pdf

The Refinery. (2021). Lifespan of Social Media Posts in 2021: How Long Do They Last? Retrieved from https://the-refinery.io/blog/how-long-does-a-social-media-post-last

Chapter 4:

Oberlo. (n.d). Facebook Age Demographics. Retrieved from https://www.oberlo.com/statistics/facebook-age-demographics#:~:text=A%20recent%20study%20analyzing%20Facebook,of%20all%20Facebook%20users%20worldwide

Omnicore. (2023). Instagram by the Numbers: Stats, Demographics & Fun Facts. Retrieved from https://www.omnicoreagency.com/instagram-statistics/#:~:text=Instagram%20Demographics,users%20are%2065%2B%20years%20old

Search Logistics. (2023). TikTok User Statistics: Everything You Need To Know About Tiktok Users. Retrieved from https://www.searchlogistics.com/learn/statistics/tiktok-user-statistics/#:~:text=TikTok%20gained%201.36%20billion%20downloads,billion%20monthly%20active%20users%20worldwide

The Social Shepherd. (2023). 21 Essential TikTok Statistics You Need to Know in 2023. Retrieved from https://thesocialshepherd.com/blog/tiktok-statistics#:~:text=TikTok%20is%20Most%20Popular%20With%20Younger%20Generations&text=Ages%2010%2D19%20are%2025,49%20is%2020.3%25%20of%20users

Money.co.uk. (2023). First-time Buyer Statistics and Facts: 2023. Retrieved from https://www.money.co.uk/mortgages/first-time-buyer-mortgages/statistics

Muck Rack. (2020). How Declining Attention Spans Impact your Social Media. Retrieved from https://muckrack.com/blog/2020/07/14/how-declining-attention-spans-impact-your-social-media

The Beat. (2022). Video Creator's Guide to YouTube's Past, Present, and Future. Retrieved from https://www.premiumbeat.com/blog/youtube-history-present-future/#:~:text=YouTube%20is%20ever%2Dchanging%2C%20whether,initiatives%2C%20and%20more%20immersive%20experiences

Shopify. (2023). How To Make Money on YouTube in 2023: 7 Simple Strategies (+ Video). https://www.shopify.com/blog/198134793-how-to-make-money-on-youtube#:~:text=To%20start%20earning%20money%20directly,Program%20and%20monetize%20your%20channel

Zippia. (2023). 20 Mobile Vs. Desktop Usage Statistics [2023]: What Percentage of Internet Traffic is Mobile? Retrieved from https://www.zippia.com/advice/mobile-vs-desktop-usage-statistics/#:~:text=Global%20Mobile%20Vs.-,Desktop%20Statistics,mobile%20phone%20at%20least%20once